THE RIVER MEDWAY

by

HOWARD BIGGS

TERENCE DALTON LIMITED
LAVENHAM . SUFFOLK
1982

Published by
TERENCE DALTON LIMITED

ISBN 0 86138 005 3

Text photoset in 11/12 pt. Baskerville

Printed in Great Britain at
THE LAVENHAM PRESS LIMITED
LAVENHAM . SUFFOLK

Contents

Index of Illustrations

To "McB" who first aroused my love of history

Introduction and Acknowledgements

FROM THE earliest habitation of this country, the valley of the River Medway and the gap by which it pierces the North Downs have been of importance. Here Neolithic man raised his great megalithic monuments such as Kit's Coty, the Iron Age people constructed their defensive hill-forts further inland; but with the advent of the Romans we find the river taking on its role as a defensive line, the Legions being delayed a full two days before they could effect a crossing by reason of the strenuous British resistance based on such a strong position.

In writing a book about a river it is only too easy to become side-tracked, to devote too much time to the historical events associated with it; or else to veer off to the other extreme and produce something in the nature of an elaborate form of guide-book. Every river of any size follows the pattern so movingly described in the melodies of Smetana's "Vltava", the swelling of cool and quiet springs in sylvan glades, the ripple of the tributaries, the sweep through undulating plains past towns, factories and cities until at last it comes to its ultimate home, the sea.

Such, too, is the Medway, but so very much more. The main waterway from the Weald of Kent, providing water-power in its upper reaches, sliding past hop-gardens and orchards and what William Cobbett refers to as "the finest seven miles I have ever seen in England, or anywhere else", the river has always provided strange contrasts. The small villages and country towns of the headwaters seem remote from the age of the M2 Motorway bridge, castles and priories are still in occupation while only a few miles away downstream huge cement works and factories hum with activity close to the sites of Roman villas. Always subject to spreading floods in winter—though less so since modern improvements and dredging have been undertaken—in summer it provides a wide estuary for yachting, with peaceful reaches above Allington for pleasure-boats, swimming or angling.

Through these pages stride the forms of the Great Alfred, Archbishop Gundulf, the tragic Anne Boleyn, the ill-fated but gallant Sir Thomas Wyatt and the Elizabethan soldier-poet Sir Philip Sidney. Here also we see Nelson joining his first ship at the age of twelve, Charles Dickens strolling the banks while living at Gad's Hill, and W. L. Wyllie, one of our greatest marine artists. Great and famous warships have been built on our river, so have ochre-sailed spritsail barges. Companies whose products have become known throughout the world or which have revolutionised aspects of modern life had their inception close to a Norman castle and to Gundulf's cathedral. Cargo vessels and pleasure steamers have threaded the waters where once lay hulks crammed with prisoners of war or convicts.

In seeking to weave together all these various strands into a coherent pattern I have found it impossible to do more than touch lightly on matters that have been dealt with in depth by many eminent writers. Like many others who have sought to portray something of our county I am above all indebted to the books and articles of the late Robert Goodsall whose knowledge of the Kentish countryside and its waterways was so exhaustive. Scholars and historians have delved into every other aspect of life in the county, every town and village along the river has its own individual story. How can one possibly do justice to them all? Readers may even find it hard to recognise their own well-known surroundings from the sometimes random facts that I have distilled. I have merely tried to embody sufficient detail to whet the reader's appetite and perhaps to open up new lines of inquiry, to help him (or her) to a fuller realisation of the beauty and fascination of the countryside through which the Medway passes, the thousand and one facets that lend it enchantment. Only briefly have I referred to the lonely and desolate wastes round about Deadman's Island which gleam their trackless and remote mudbanks within sight of the mighty oil refinery on the Isle of Grain, the great super-tankers lying at the end of their jetties to unload, the new power-station not far away.

Seeking information I have approached many individuals and organisations, and I would like to record here the great debt of gratitude I owe to Viscount Astor and to Viscount De L'Isle and Dudley, V.C., both of whom so kindly read through and amended the sections on their historic homes. Many others whom I approached were also most helpful, especially the staffs of the various Public Libraries and Museums who took endless trouble in turning up what I required. It would be impossible to list all those to whom I am indebted but I would like to mention particularly the assistance given me by the following:- The Association of Men of Kent and Kentish Men, H. R. Balston, Gordon Beech, Rev. R. C. Bell of Hollingbourne, *Bleak House* archives, R. Corben, Alan Cordell, The County Archivist, Crescent Shipping, G. Harvey of the Medway Military Research Group, Mrs G. Hodge, Tony Kremer, J. P. Knight Ltd., Jack Lacey of *Medport News*, W. H. Lapthorne, Clive Lawford my special photographer, Leeds Castle Foundation, Mid-Kent Water Authority, Maritime Trust, Patricia O'Driscoll, E. D. G. Payne, J. M. Preston, The Prior of Aylesford, Rochester Bridge Wardens, R. J. Spain, Society for Spritsail Barge Research, R. A. Stevens and Colonel J. M. Wilson. There are many others who have turned up items of information, printed off photographs or assisted in so many ways. To all of them I would like to extend my grateful thanks; and more particularly to my wife whose busy typewriter has recorded nearly every word of this book and who has shared with me in all the excitements of this quest.

HOWARD BIGGS

Broadstairs.
February 1982.

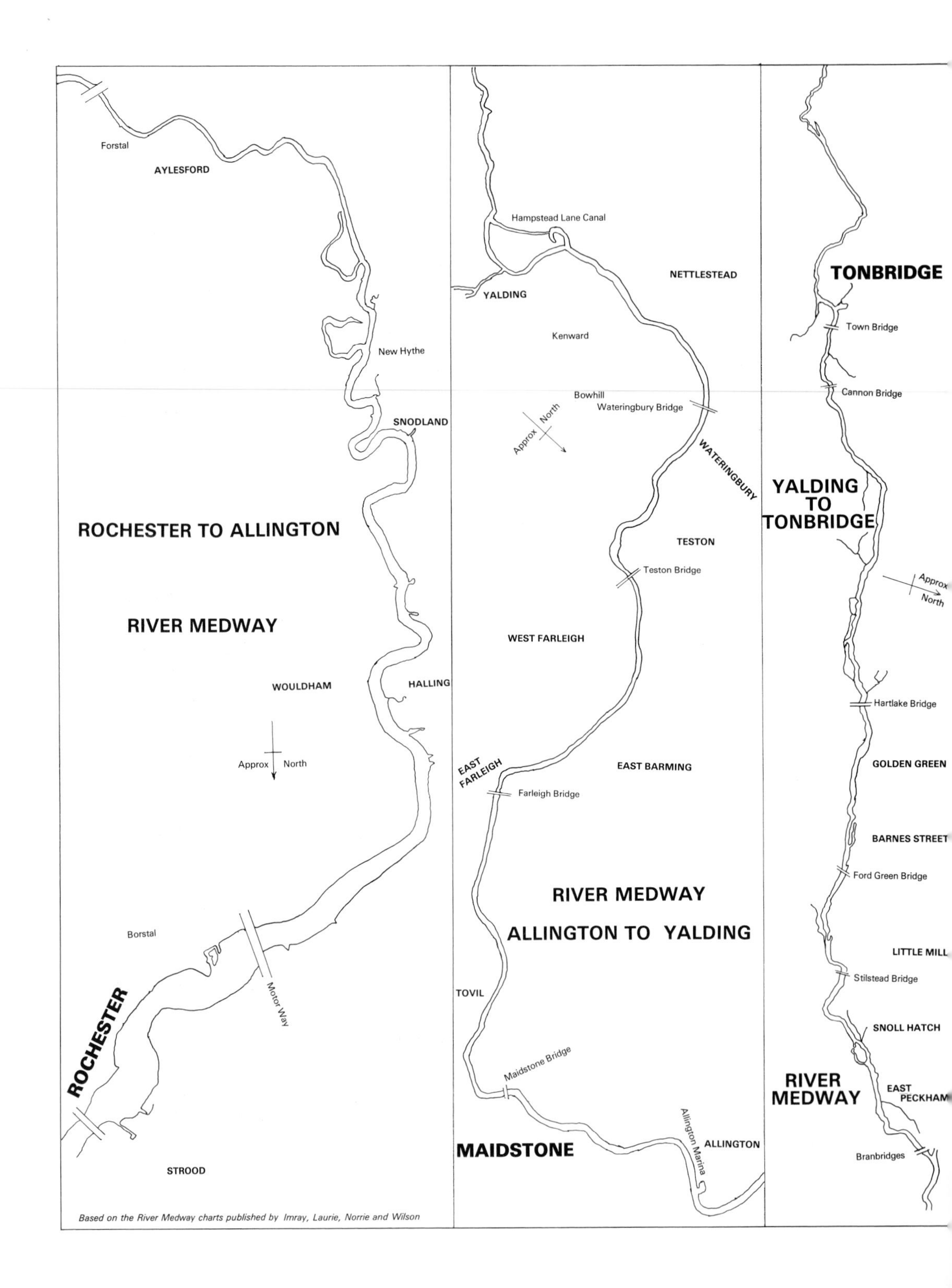

Forstal
AYLESFORD
New Hythe
SNODLAND
ROCHESTER TO ALLINGTON
RIVER MEDWAY
WOULDHAM
HALLING
Approx North
Borstal
Motor Way
ROCHESTER
STROOD
Based on the River Medway charts published by Imray, Laurie, Norrie and Wilson
Hampstead Lane Canal
YALDING
NETTLESTEAD
Kenward
Bowhill
Wateringbury Bridge
Approx North
WATERINGBURY
TESTON
Teston Bridge
WEST FARLEIGH
EAST FARLEIGH
EAST BARMING
Farleigh Bridge
RIVER MEDWAY
ALLINGTON TO YALDING
TOVIL
Maidstone Bridge
Allington Marina
MAIDSTONE
ALLINGTON
TONBRIDGE
Town Bridge
Cannon Bridge
YALDING TO TONBRIDGE
Approx North
Hartlake Bridge
GOLDEN GREEN
BARNES STREET
Ford Green Bridge
LITTLE MILL
Stilstead Bridge
SNOLL HATCH
RIVER MEDWAY
EAST PECKHAM
Branbridges

CHAPTER ONE

Men of Kent and Kentish Men

THE STORY of a river is like a biography, with the additional dimension of the record of thousands of years instead of the normal life-span. Where then should a start be made? Is the birth in time or in place? Whichever is chosen it can be possible to mention only key features and events, their impact on local and national history, and the people affected. But even this would produce an immense volume if all the characters, their deeds and misdeeds were fully traced and analysed.

The Medway which flows from its source in the Ashdown Forest area of East Sussex in, very roughly, a north-easterly direction, through Tonbridge, Maidstone and Rochester to the sea, is not at first sight dramatic. It cannot match—or so it would appear—the swift-flowing becks of the Pennine country or the cascading streams of the Lake District which, after only a day or so of heavy rain, will turn into foaming torrents, plucking and tearing at banks and boulders. The upper stretches, above Allington Lock near Maidstone which is the limit of the tidal stream, have a normally slow flow, somewhere in the region of two and a half knots; it appears what might be called "canalised" and orderly, with a tow-path for the seventeen miles between Tonbridge and Maidstone, the banks mainly grass-covered stones, and with locks at intervals of about two miles or so. The tidal reaches between Allington Lock and the sea are industrialised. However the river as a whole is attractive and full of interest, with an infinite variety of rural scenery in its seventy miles, much of it as yet unspoiled.

But this quietness is just one of the many contrasts of this fascinating river. A quick glance through the records of the town of Tonbridge, nearly at the head of the navigable waterway, shows how frequently that area has been affected by floods, parts of the High Street being inundated over and over again. Further down stream Edward Hasted mentions in his topographical survey of the county how the river would rise as much as eighteen feet after forty-eight hours of heavy rain, this rendering Teston and East Farleigh bridges entirely impassable. There are records of ice-floes, after a period of hard frost, crunching over the parapet of Teston Bridge, the water beneath the ice submerging the piers and arches and swirling along past East Farleigh and finally spilling over the much larger bridge at Maidstone. All this is in the area above Allington Lock and so unaffected by the ebb and flow of tides; but before this lock was constructed in 1792 the tide ran up to East Farleigh, a further four and a half miles, which increased the risk of flooding considerably.

All these references are to more or less recent times. Much further back in the history of this country, when the waters from north and south indundated the low-lying land between us and Europe, thus forming the English Channel (about 10,000 B.C.) and the only inhabitants were the wandering hunters of the Old Stone Age, the Medway river was vigorously at work, carving its way deeper and deeper through the chalk hills of the North Downs, seeking its outlet to the sea. Gravel and small stones which it had gouged out on its way were hurried towards the sea; for in those far-off days it was wider than the Thames and had an even swifter flow. But, as is shown in the Geological Survey of 1954 which is quoted by Patrick Thornhill in *Archaeologia Cantiana* (*LXXXIX*), with the rise of the sea the river flow slackened and the gravel was deposited to form the river bed.

During the course of several thousand years, in Mesolithic times, its width contracted, it began to wind to and fro and deposit silt on top of the gravel. So to-day we have the river flowing between its orderly banks, much of the bed between Allington Lock and the sea being deep mud; yet well beneath this layer, which is in places as much as twenty feet thick, is the "buried channel", the evidence of the Medway's earlier vigour. This is the area of the "Medway Gap", the cleft in the North Downs, which can be so clearly made out in a north-easterly direction from the A20 at West Malling. Better still there are spectacular views of it from the Medway motorway bridge on the M2 and from the train as it climbs up what the railmen call the "Chatham Bank" on the way to London.

At Forest Row the sylvan streamlet gains the strength that cleft the North Downs.
Clive Lawford

Another distinctive feature of this part is the group of Megalithic tombs clustered in the neighbourhood of Addington and Aylesford, at the south-western end of the Gap, and dating from somewhere between 2500 and 2000 B.C. Altogether it is estimated that there are some two thousand known tombs of this age in the British Isles, but nearly one thousand of these are in Ireland and most of the others are in the hillier areas. But there are notable exceptions, among them the well-known East and West Kennet barrows near Avebury in Wiltshire, and this isolated group in Kent.

All these Medway tombs seem to be of roughly similar pattern, having a simple rectangular chamber at the eastern end of the mound, some kind of a forecourt, and the chamber formed by upstanding blocks of Sarsen stone with a cap-stone. Kit's Coty is the most famous of these, the existing uprights and cap being apparently an additional or false doorway; but there are five others as well as the "Countless Stones", all marking the burial sites of members of a family, or tribe, perhaps. In the case of the "Chestnuts" at Addington, reported by Dr John Alexander in *Archaeologia Cantiana* (*LXXVI*), the mound was 64 feet wide by 50 feet long and there were the remains of ten bodies within together with a scattering of flint flakes. Later in Neolithic times cremations took place here and to judge from the variety of pottery the tomb was in use over a considerable period of time in New Stone and Early Bronze Ages. It is a mistake, I think, to become too involved in detailed archaeological research but the great impact of these impressive stones, most of them near the line of the ancient Pilgrims' Way, is the knowledge that men and women have dwelt here in this Medway valley, fashioning tools or weapons, farming,

The famous stones at Kit's Coty.
Author's collection

seeking their food and finding shelter continuously over these thousands of years. And how did they come here? To the west lay the wet clays of the Wealden forest, marshy and impenetrable. Many of the traces in the tombs and settlements, flint flakes, types of pottery and the form of construction are closely linked with other rather similar tombs and settlements along the Atlantic coast of Brittany dating back to around 2000 B.C., and so it seems likely that they must have journeyed up the river from the sea. Later, in about 1800 B.C., came the Beaker-people from the Rhine-mouth with their knowledge of the use of metals, particularly bronze and copper, and it is clear that there was a certain exchange of trade even as far back as that—and all of it up the River Medway.

So far this biography has been concentrated on the Medway Gap for only in the few hundred years before the coming of the Romans was there any settlement higher up the river. And here we find a very strange thing, a distinction referred to even to-day, between the people living in Eastern Kent and those to the West of the river, the "Men of Kent" and the "Kentish Men". The people who settled here in the second and third centuries B.C. were of Belgic race, a far more civilised people, who seem to have adopted the river as a definite political frontier between different tribes, according to examples of coinages discovered; it was only the threat of Roman invasion which brought a temporary link between them.

As will be explained later, the settlers to the east of the Medway, the Men of Kent, in due course developed customs, laws and a way of life quite distinct from those living to the west of the river. But both groups share a pride in Kent which has led to the establishment of County Societies. The first recorded was a Society of Men of Kent in 1657 to which Kentish Men were admitted the following year. However, this was during the Commonwealth and with Cromwell's death causing great political upheaval it is uncertain how long this Society survived. In 1696, as we read in the present Society's journal it was revived as "A feast for the County of Kent" and held annually till 1701. The present "Men of Kent and Kentish Men" started its life in the Holborn Viaduct Hotel, London, in 1897 and from that time it has thrived greatly, holding meetings, concerts and other activities as well as being a philanthropic organisation.

There is no need to refer in detail to Caesar's two reconnaissance expeditions; the first in 55 B.C. lasting 24 days when he only penetrated some 12 miles inland from Walmer, the second the following year when he remained four months, advancing as far as St Albans and withdrawing with hostages and a promise of tribute money. As a result of these forays he regarded this land of Cantium or Kent as a more civilised and prosperous region than any other. During the ensuing ninety-seven years, while the Romans were stabilising their position and settlement in Northern France (or

Massive walls of the Roman defensive fortress at Richborough, one of the Saxon Shore forts.
Author's collection

Gaul), the tribes of the Medway area were in close contact with their fellow Belgae in the Pas-de-Calais; a Gallo-Belgic gold stater or coin of this period found in the Medway marshes at Upchurch in 1967 is a symbol of this contact. The main tribal centre on the river was Rochester, a town important enough to have a local mint and undoubtedly a place well known to Roman merchants who all this time carried on a brisk trade between the continent and Britain.

When the invasion was finally mounted in 43 A.D. and Aulus Plautius landed at Richborough with his four legions, the famous IInd Augusta, and the XXth Valeria Victrix among them, the local rulers Caractacus and Togodumnus were taken by surprise as there had previously been one or two false alarms. They made a tentative resistance beyond Canterbury, realised that the invading force was massive, well-trained and efficient, and so after one or two skirmishes, retired behind the Medway to muster their forces. The fords, where the Pilgrims' Way crossed the river, were obvious danger spots so without doubt some defences were set up there; but all the evidence of Latin writers points to Rochester as the scene of the crucial engagement. The Britons built strongly fortified positions on the north west bank, trenched the ford and held their chariots in reserve. The Roman legions came rolling on remorselessly, and, while slingers and javelin throwers prowled the banks, a large party of Batavian auxiliary troops used to swimming fully armed, slid across undetected, wreaking havoc among the chariots and horses as they made a surprise attack upon the encampment. Under cover of this confusion further legionaries crossed the river by raft, forming a secure bridge-head on the far bank. At low tide rubble and stones were added to the ford to enable the full strength of the Roman army to be deployed. Meanwhile a flank attack was made by units of the IInd legion under Vespasian who crossed further up-stream at the nearest shallow place—possibly Snodland or Aylesford. So, on the second day, a massive assault by forces under Hosidius Geta settled the matter, and the Britons withdrew in the direction of the River Thames.

This was the most important engagement of the whole campaign for though there was stiff resistance in the Thames marshes and at the Brentwood ridge on the way to Colchester the experience gained by Aulus Plautius in overcoming a determined opponent at this natural barrier of the Medway brought him ultimate victory.

It is interesting to note that on several occasions since, the Medway has been regarded as a major defensive line. There were Norman castles, of course, at Rochester, Allington and Tonbridge, but these were more for the purpose of keeping the surrounding people in order. The river provided a difficult crossing both for William Rufus and for King John when they attacked Rochester Castle as will be seen in Chapter Nine. Elizabeth I established Chatham dockyard and therefore had to build Upnor Castle just below as a defence. Later still during the wars with France in the eighteenth century it was suggested that the flooding of all the upper reaches would provide a most useful barrier against invading troops; and even in the Second World War a similar plan for flooding the Medway was put forward by Sir Winston Churchill which, with concrete defence blockhouses, would provide some additional problems for invading panzer divisions.

After the Romans had brought the *Pax Romana* to these shores and the country was becoming increasingly prosperous, several villas were built along the banks of the Medway above Rochester. Just like the manors of later date, these were generally the centre of an estate, with numerous lesser farms and small-holdings associated with them: the wealth and importance of the owner can usually be judged by the type of villa, whether the rooms open one into another, or whether there is a corridor; whether it had bath rooms incorporated in the villa or separate bath-houses; and whether there were mosaic decorations in any of the rooms.

I have already stressed that the Medway Gap has an exceptional group of Megalithic tombs; now we have another remarkable feature for one of the Roman villas located in this neighbourhood, that at Eccles, was found to have a complete suite of nineteen rooms connected with the baths dating back to the first century A.D., within a very few years of the Roman invasion. Furthermore the cold room (frigidarium) and its plunge-bath were floored with mosaic pavement. This is only one of three villas discovered in the whole country to have had mosaics and an elaborate bathing system built as early as this; which seems to indicate a remarkable degree of Romanisation operating here. The cold room floor had what appears to be a gladiator motif, while the plunge-bath appropriately had a dolphin pattern on the bottom; this one room measured about 19 feet by 29 feet 6 inches which is large for a room in a private house.

Another of the rooms, the hot room, was 32 feet by 12 feet 6 inches; and in yet another which must have contained a hot plunge-bath there was evidence of the metal tank or testudo which, being set over the furnace, provided a circulation of hot water. All these discoveries recorded by Mr A. P. Detsicas make fascinating reading in the volumes of *Archaeologia Cantiana* from 1963 onward.

One can imagine the standard of living, the state of civilisation that would require such a bath complex drawing the water from the river, and all this nineteen hundred years ago. Traces have been found of other villas through the Medway Gap and up the river at Maidstone and beyond. The whole of this area became well settled, particularly along the line of the Roman road noted by I. D. Margary which ran from Watling Street at Rochester to Maidstone and then along the foot of the Chart hills to Lympne. Some of the Roman foundations are of doubtful purpose, like the traces of a kind of vaulted cellar discovered alongside the river at Burham in 1895. At first thought to be a temple to the God Mithras, the later discovery of piles in the river bank suggested rather a wharf and storage cellar in which jars of oil or best Falernian wine might be stood after a voyage up-river in a merchant ship. There might be problems about the size of ship, though, for the Romans very soon built a bridge across the Medway at Rochester to carry what was later known as Watling Street, the piles of which were discovered by later builders, and the low head-room would have necessitated careful choice of tide.

The biography of this river in its infant years has still concentrated on the Gap thus far, but now we can spread our gaze further afield as we have reached a time of prosperity, with trade flowing up and down stream; for we know that in the Britain of Roman times there was a considerable export trade in corn, cattle, hunting dogs, jet, and metals such as gold, tin and iron. The pre-Roman tracks, winter routes high on the hill-ridges, summer ways along the foot-hills, frequently added miles to a journey by their circuitous routes. But the business-like Romans who particularly required roads to move legions from place to place in a hurry, to speed messengers on their way, or to maintain efficient contact between important towns began to develop a carefully devised system infinitely better than these ancient ways which, even on downland, could become impassable quagmires in wet weather. For this reason, too, it is obvious that they would have used the river where possible, for much of the surrounding country in the upper reaches was thickly wooded. The further west towards the Weald one proceeded, the denser grew the trees for this was the great Andredswald, the forest principally of oak whose sparse remnants are now referred to as Ashdown Forest.

In this area, deep in the forest, the Romans established a thriving iron mining industry, digging out the clay ironstone and burning or smelting it with local timber as fuel. The rather impure wrought iron thus produced could be forged into implements immediately or else hammered into a solid mass known as bloom, while the clinker and cinder waste materials were frequently used as road-surfacing for the ways serving the iron-making area. The Roman road running from Rochester to Maidstone and then on to Lympne forked about five miles south-east of Maidstone passing right across the iron-working zone of the Weald and ending up at Hastings; there was another road, too, from the iron district stretching through Benenden, Tenterden, Ashford and so to Canterbury.

From the first Roman occupation until the early years of the third century defence against invaders was the task of garrison troops. Then Saxon pirates, from the German coast, set out to loot the rich towns and villas in Britain. As a result an officer, the Count of the Saxon Shore, was specially appointed to ward off these attacks and for this purpose he had under his command a chain of forts with their necessary garrisons and anchorages for the fleet on the coasts of Norfolk, Suffolk, Essex and Kent. Units of the famous IInd Legion Augusta were stationed at Richborough, one of the most famous of the Shore forts, but by about 410 the troops were recalled for the defence of Italy and even Rome itself and the people of Britain had to cope with the Saxon incursions as best they could.

It seems incredible that the country could have reached such a considerable stage of civilisation under the Romans and then have slipped back into chaos soon after they left. Perhaps very largely this was due to the methods adopted by successive Roman Governors of the Province, from Agricola (70 A.D.) onwards, to encourage the local tribes to administer their own laws and customs under their own ruler. So, when the legions departed, there was no supreme leader in the fight against the invaders. The legendary Arthur may have been one such leader, carrying on resistance in the West; but here, in Kent, the local King Vortigern was in the fore-front of defence. The well-known story of his invitation to a band of Jutish warriors under Hengist and Horsa to help him drive out other invaders is based on the *Anglo-Saxon Chronicle*; and these warriors were granted the Isle of

Countless stones
Author's Collection

Cross erected at Ebbsfleet in 1897 to mark the landing of St Augustine in 597.
Author's collection

Thanet as a recompense for their help. Unhappily something went wrong with the arrangement, the warriors fixed greedy eyes on mainland Kent and soon, about 451 A.D., Vortigern and his son Catigern were involved in a desperate battle in which supposedly both Horsa and Catigern were slain. One of the Sarsen stones near Kit's Coty is known as the "White Horse Stone" and the story is that on this spot Hengist proudly raised his victorious banner bearing the white horse, from which Kent takes its county emblem.

There is much folk-lore and legend connected with all this; even the site of the final battle is uncertain being mentioned by Bede as "on the plain near the sea in the place of the inscribed stone". However what is indisputable is that Hengist's warriors over-ran Kent, the Romano-British, those that survived, withdrew to the West; and where Christianity had flourished as one of the religions of the later Roman Empire the whole land passed into the heathen embrace of Woden and Thor while the Medway was watching and brooding on all these startling events.

But who were these people; where did they originate—these people that Bede refers to as Jutes? They seem to have been quite a separate group of adventurers from the Saxons and the available evidence indicates that they settled in only three parts of the British Isles, here in Kent, in the Isle of Wight and down the Meon valley in Hampshire.

The main sources which give us information about these people are the burials; they believed that the dead would need those items they normally used in their daily life on earth, in Valhalla. The pottery vessels, ornaments and weapons which have come to light indicate that they were probably Frankish tribesmen from the middle reaches of the River Rhine, and this is borne out by the unique laws and customs which were established here by them: the status of the freeman of the tribe, the way in which the administration of the territory was divided up into a number of so-called lathes or provinces, the strange law of inheritance known as Gavelkind (by which all sons inherited in equal shares), and the manner in which the tribesmen settled down in more or less scattered and isolated farms and hamlets as opposed to a united group in a village. All these features are common both to East Kent and to the Franks of the Rhine but are not known anywhere else in England; also there are a number of place-names in Kent which show a similar link. These were the Men of Kent.

This individual quality in Kent was maintained by the great King Ethelbert who, in spite of a defeat by the West Saxons, was able through his personality and wisdom to raise his county to a pre-eminent position during his long reign of fifty-six years (560-616), being acknowledged as leader and overlord by all the Saxon Kings in the southern part of the land.

It was to this noble King that Pope Gregory the Great sent St Augustine, and in 597 he landed at Ebbesfleet in the Pegwell Bay area, soon afterward baptising the King himself. So Christianity returned to Kent first, St Augustine became the first Archbishop of Canterbury and head of the Christian Church here; while Ethelbert was still reigning, a second diocese was established on the river at Rochester in 604, a certain Justus who had been sent by the Pope to help St Augustine being nominated as Bishop. This very early re-establishment of Christianity also marks out Kent as unique; neighbouring tribes of Saxons were still heathen some sixty years later, but of course this was due to some extent to the very slight contact the men of Kent had with tribes of different origin. Also the heavy clay soil of the Weald and the impenetrable forest of Anderida provided a distinct barrier. That this was so can be seen from the number of Jutish placenames recorded in the Medway and River Len areas, while there are no early names in the Wealden district. Only much later, in the eighth and ninth centuries do any names occur in the Weald, these chiefly dens and hursts (i.e. a clearing for pigs and wooded hillocks).

The final stage in this first part of this biography introduces the courageous figure of King Alfred—and, naturally, his resistance to the Danes; and this links up neatly with the question of place-names for as F. W. Jessup tells, in his *Kent History Illustrated*, there are no Danish names in Kent. Nonetheless, from the moment their long-ships first threatened the South Coast in 787, the Vikings were an ever-present danger. At first they made sporadic raids, bent on plunder; but gradually these became more frequent and the loss and destruction greater. In 842 there were disastrous attacks on Canterbury and Rochester, then in 850 a band of Vikings actually set up some kind of a winter quarters in Thanet, following this up four years later by a similar winter sojourn in Sheppey at Medway mouth. From this it was clear that, though their initial aim was to loot the towns and particularly the abbeys and monasteries, the ultimate intention was one of colonisation, to found a Norse settlement in our land. From 865 onward great Danish hosts swept down on the East Anglian seaboard and gradually began to settle there and all up the north-east coast of Britain. When Alfred became King of Wessex in 871, he had no less than nine major battles with the Danes in his first year; and in spite of his great victory of Ethandune and subsequent peace treaty with the Danish leader Guthrum, there were other Viking bands roving the seas who took no notice of treaties of any kind and would invade and over-run where they could. Now came the proof of Alfred's wisdom in establishing a regular army and starting to build up a navy; for when another attack was made on Rochester in 884 he was able to force the Danes to retreat leaving the town unharmed. The Vikings withdrew in their long-ships and for a while turned their attentions to northern France where they were allowed to colonise Normandy in much the same way as Alfred had permitted the settlers in the north and east of England to remain, himself being supreme overlord of the whole country. Alfred, however, was not deceived by an apparent quietness and when another Danish onslaught under Haesten took place in 892 he was ready from his main centre near Milton Regis to cut off any marauding bands. At length this force, too, was dispersed and Haesten withdrew into the Danish part of Eastern England.

Now that we have reached the years of the Norman Conquest we can turn our eyes away from the Medway Gap to all the upper reaches of the river, for with an increasing population the Weald was becoming more settled, estates and manors were being established in suitable places, and beside tributary streams, the Medway as we know it today was being born.

Kentish White Horse — *Kent County Council*

CHAPTER TWO

The Shadow of Tudor Monarchs

THE SOURCE of the Medway lies in the great iron-working area along the Kent and Sussex border. This river, which carved its way so vigorously through the land in earlier times when it neared the sea, rises along the Forest Ridge in Ashdown Forest, surely one of the most beautiful parts of Sussex.

Its head-waters occur at Turner's Hill, or actually, as R. H. Goodsall describes in his book on the Medway, in Butcher's Wood. There is a watershed here, the source of the Ouse is close to hand, but the infant Medway winds along to the north of the Forest Ridge, past Forest Row and along the little valley rich in water meadows and pasture to Hartfield before it swings away northward into Kent.

Only about two miles away another river, the Eden, starts on its journey to join the Medway at Penshurst; for many miles the two rivers flow on more or less parallel courses, all the while being joined by lesser streams which, at some point in their flow, have been dammed off into ponds—many of which still exist—to provide water-power for mills, or hammers connected with the forging of iron.

The market town of Edenbridge was the site of the historic crossing of the River Eden by Roman road and possibly by prehistoric track. No trace remains of the Roman bridge which may have been of wood but more likely was of stone, however there are certainly records of a stone bridge here in Tudor times. The present one, much altered and adapted, dates from 1830 and is a modern structure compared with the ancient timbered buildings, many of the fifteenth, sixteenth, or seventeenth centuries, which line the main street. The Crown Inn, "Ye Olde Crown", is another fine old timbered building, with massive gateway and a secret passage used by smugglers in days gone by; for this was on the road between London and Lewes with its direct connection with the wooded dells and hiding-places of the Weald.

A prosperous place in medieval times, Edenbridge was the essential crossing place for goods from the Wealden iron furnaces, but it was also the centre of a sheep-farming area. Mills for grinding corn grown on local arable land were built in the town, one of which, Haxted Mill, survives a short distance away though now as a mill museum. Between the seventeenth and nineteenth centuries its prosperity declined with the removal of the iron industry and weaving to the Midlands; but latterly its proximity to the capital has brought renewed prosperity.

When the Roman Legions left, the iron industry, a valuable export, along with the other signs of civilised living, the baths with their iron hot-water tanks and the villas with their under-floor central heating, became neglected. The Jutes with their utterly different kind of life ignored the iron-stone but made use of the Roman roads, with their hard surface of slag and clinker from the old iron-workings, passing along them with their herds of swine to pasture in the depth of the Wealden forest.

All this the waters of the Medway saw; and noticed too the faint glimmerings of a re-awakening interest by a recording of an iron-working at East Grinstead in the Domesday Survey.

It was many years, though, before a full-scale industry had re-established itself; but then, with the iron-stone and the timber for smelting so conveniently together, the stream handy to provide water-power to drive bellows to increase the heat of the charcoal fuel and work the hammers which would convert the very imperfect bloom into wrought iron, the increase was rapid. The first bellows-type forge is mentioned as being at Newbridge near Hartfield in about 1496. By the time that the awe-inspiring figure of Henry VIII was paying his court to the young Anne Boleyn at Hever, the range of iron articles was extensive—anything from horse-shoes to the iron rims of cart-wheels, cannon, a few examples of which are outside the Tower of London, iron fire-backs and grave-slabs; and, at a later date, railings for St Paul's Cathedral manufactured at Lamberhurst. During Queen Elizabeth's reign a list was compiled showing some 115 sites, but after this the industry started to decline, the use of coal and coke for smelting in the Midlands ultimately putting an end to it. The last forge was at Ashburnham in Sussex which closed in 1828.

These upper waters of the Medway, merely streams in reality, were sufficient to provide a good head of water, when dammed in the ponds, to drive the required machinery. (Much further information about the details of this industry can be found in E. W. Straker's fascinating book *Wealden Iron.*) However in the lower reaches, as will be seen later, the river ultimately provided a splendid route for timber and cannon to be transported to the Royal dockyards at Chatham and Sheerness at a time when the roads were still impossibly bad.

So, in a most unusual degree, the contrasting nature of the Medway manifests itself. The headwaters were the early source of power for industry but now the area is rich in agriculture. Timber and cannon once floated down it for ships of war, passing through a landscape of peaceful husbandry where now motor cruisers and small pleasure craft slice the reflecting surface; the figures of kings and queens, nobles and ladies, join the iron-masters in the pageant of history.

It would be impossible to enumerate the many fine mansions, the fourteenth and fifteenth century churches that abound, without turning this into a guide book, nor to record the numerous famous characters linked with the river.

Mention must be made, however, of the tiny and attractive village of Chiddingstone with its row of charming old houses with typical sixteenth century half-timbering in Wealden oak which are now cared for by the National Trust. Not far away is the massive block of sandstone known as the "Chiding Stone" around which many stories have gathered and which is supposed to have given its name to the village, a most unlikely derivation. In the sandstone Church of St Mary is an iron-slab memorial to an iron-master, Richard Streatfeild, who died in 1601, a member of a respected local family; the name lives on for it was a Sir Henry Streatfeild who sold the estate in 1932. Near here also, at Chiddingstone Causeway, is the cricket ball factory founded by the Duke family, which will be mentioned later.

This particular iron grave-slab is supposed to have been cast at Cowden where there were iron workings in Tudor times operated by Quyntyn and Weston, Furnace Farm reminding us of this; and there again in the church is another of these iron grave slabs. Also, very close to Cowden, passes one of the Roman roads used for moving iron down to the coast. Right through until Stuart times these clinker and slag-metalled roads, carved through the Wealden country by the Legions, were the principal highways; for the raised mound or agger on which they were built, the well-packed surface and the pronounced camber which drained away all surface water made them far superior to the mud and pot-hole tracks that passed for medieval roads. At Holtye, very near to Furnace Farm, a stretch of the Roman road was uncovered where the slag surface still showed the grooves worn by Roman cart-wheels, mute reminder of the industry that once thrived in this now "green and pleasant land" of water meadows and little folds of hills.

Such iron goods, in Tudor and Stuart times, as were not sent northward might well be moved to ports like Meeching Haven, later Newhaven, at the mouth of the Ouse, or to the Cinque Ports of Rye and Winchelsea for transit to France. Also the "owlers", the smugglers of Romney Marsh in the time of the first Elizabeth or the early Stuarts dealt not only in contraband wool, liquor from France or the later popular tobacco and tea. Even stranger cargoes were "run", when iron cannon were hidden beneath ostensibly peaceful goods, or quantities of Fuller's earth were illegally exported. Judge the difficulty of smuggling sufficient of this latter dusty clay substance to France or to the Low Countries to make it worth while running the risk!

As the ever-increasing waters of the Medway and its tributary the Eden draw nearer to each other, and the Kent Water comes in to meet them from the centre, this lozenge of well-farmed countryside contains two of the most

In the upper reaches — water meadows and a weir. *Clive Lawford*

interesting and absorbing buildings in a county unusually rich in such historic structures. W. S. Shears makes special reference to the castles and manor houses of Kent in *This England*, and of these surely two of the most famous must be Hever Castle and Penshurst Place. Around both of them the formidable Henry VIII strode; Penshurst was his possession for a time and his visits to Hever were many, his approach heralded by the sounding of a horn from some nearby hilltop as he rode in to visit Sir Thomas Bullen — or Boleyn — and his attractive daughter Anne.

The Castle of Hever itself is on the banks of the River Eden. Starting first as a small farm or manor house defended by a moat in the thirteenth century, it developed gradually into something stronger and more imposing as licences were granted to add crenellations. From behind this upjutting stonework watchful archers could keep safe the property in the war-like days when King Edward III was embarking on his adventures at Calais. With William de Hever's inheritance passing to daughters, Sir John de Cobham, husband of the elder, obtained possession and he again added further battlements. His memorial dated 1380 is in Hever Church.

During the following turbulent half century starting with the advent of Sir John Fastolf, who was reputedly the original for Shakespeare's Falstaff, the house passed into several ownerships until at length a friend and business associate of Sir John's, one Sir Geoffrey Bullen, purchased it. This Sir Geoffrey was of good Norfolk family, a mercer by trade who had been Lord Mayor of London some three years before he bought Hever. Very probably, like the previous three owners, he intended it more as an investment than as a dwelling place, for he also owned Blickling Hall in his own home county of Norfolk. Nevertheless, as it was only some 25 miles from London it would provide an admirable retreat where Sir Geoffrey could ride the country and relax from the cares of business. His son William, who inherited in 1464, used it as his seat; so, after years of intermittent usage, at length this fortified manor became a dwelling, a family home, and the eldest son Thomas, who next inherited, brought as his bride to Hever Elizabeth Howard, daughter of the second Duke of Norfolk.

Now the great days of this house beside the River Eden were about to begin. Sir Thomas was as ambitious as his father and grandfather, the lure of power and position gleamed before his eyes. Already by his marriage he had taken the first tentative steps upon the ladder of history; he held various royal appointments, was sent on an embassy to the court of the Holy Roman Emperor Maximilian, was Ambassador to France, and was present at the "Field of the Cloth of Gold", that astonishing spectacular when Henry VIII

Hever Castle, formal garden.
Clive Lawford

Henry VIII being welcomed by Sir Thomas Bullen. Anne Boleyn watches from an upstairs window.
By courtesy of Lord Astor

and Francis I of France vied with each other in brilliant retinue and glittering display and which brought no political gain whatsoever.

Yet all the time it was to Hever that Thomas returned between royal appointments, here his three children spent their childhood, and of course because of his position it was understandable that the two girls Mary and Anne should have been absorbed into the royal household. Mary was soon Lady-in-Waiting to Queen Catherine of Aragon, during which time she received particular favour from the King. Anne went to Paris with the King's sister and there completed her education. Then, when her sister Mary Bullen—with the King's approval or perhaps even at his instigation—married William Carey, Anne became the centre of Henry's interest.

All this was greatly to Sir Thomas' advantage. He became Treasurer of the Royal Household, no easy position even for an adept business man with such a prodigal king. However, he must have done well as he was soon a Knight of the Garter, was created Viscount Rochford and soon afterward Earl of Wiltshire and Earl of Ormonde.

As Maid-of-Honour to Queen Catherine Anne was the centre of attraction for many of the young nobles at court, but their attentions only increased Henry's desire. Not only did he see her at court but frequently came down to Hever. How strange to think that where these two strolled intimately beside the

Penshurst Place. Baron's Hall and visitors' entrance. *Clive Lawford*

River Eden, some four hundred and forty years later the river in furious spate should flood the ground floor rooms of the castle.

Here, perhaps, Henry determined on the plan which should make Anne his wife and Queen — if only he could arrange a divorce from Catherine. So the well-known schemes evolved, manoevres that led directly to the disgrace and death of the high and mighty Cardinal, Thomas Wolsey, the meteoric rise to high office of Dr Thomas Cranmer, the true lovers' knots emblazoned on the walls of Hampton Court Palace — and indirectly to the establishment of the Protestant Church in England. The tragic years unfolded. Henry made Anne his Queen on 1st June, she bore him not the son he so much desired but a daughter. Not quite three years later, charged with adultery and condemned for High Treason, she was brought to the scaffold in the Tower of London on 19th May 1536 and was there beheaded by a swordsman specially brought over from Calais for the purpose. Her brief exciting spell as Queen was over, her body buried hurriedly in the Chapel of St Peter ad Vincula in the Tower. Her daughter, of course, was to become in due time that great Queen Elizabeth whom heroic and far-sighted statesmen, soldiers and sea-dogs were proud to serve.

Sir Thomas Boleyn and his wife remained at Hever in obscurity till their deaths in 1537 and 1538 whereupon it passed to the King, who established there his fourth Queen, Anne of Cleves. She resided in the castle from 1540 until her death seventeen years later. Granted by Queen Mary to Sir Edward Waldegrave it remained with this family for one hundred years before slowly

Penshurst Place. *Clive Lawford*

becoming less and less important, less cared for, in parts even ruinous. The abode of queens had become no more than a working farm-house, chambers that had witnessed their lives and loves were given over to the ordinary scenes of everyday life, in place of armour and armoury were scythes, sickles and the inevitable hoe.

Finally in 1903 it was rescued by Mr William Waldorf Astor from America who set in hand, regardless of expense, the great restoration and improvement that has led to the beautiful castle and gardens of today, together with the adjoining rooms* forming the Tudor village. Since that date it has remained in the Astor family, lovingly cared for and managed as their home and the centre of a thriving estate.

Unfortunately, the fearful floods of 15th September 1968 caused appalling damage. With more than five inches of rain in sixteen hours in the immediate neighbourhood of the castle and over seven inches a short way upstream, the flood defences which had been strengthened after an inundation just ten years before proved incapable of coping with a flow of 7,000 cubic feet per second coming down the river. The whole ground floor was flooded to a depth of four and a half feet, and furniture, furnishings, everything had to be dried out, cleaned or replaced. Not until 1978 was this work of restoration completed, but done it was and the same year the Hever Castle gardens recorded the millionth visitor since they were first opened in 1965. So in 1981 Hever is home for the second Baron Astor, his lady and five children, a fitting residence for the Lord Lieutenant of the County.

*A range of connected guest-rooms which have the outward appearance of single-storey cottages.

How interesting and appropriate it is that another great and historic building in this neighbourhood should also have had close connection with the Tudor kings and queens. Yet here, at Penshurst Place, is a further instance of the contrast that is so apparent with the Medway and its tributaries. While Hever was for a while a focus of interest in the middle of the sixteenth century and then languished in comparative obscurity, passing through many hands till its recent restoration, Penshurst Place lives with tradition and with a continuity of family interest through from the time when Henry VIII's son Edward presented it to his "trustye and well-beloved servant" Sir William Sidney in 1552.

Among the Lords of Penshurst have been many prominent servants of the realm, the first recorded owner in 1299, Sir Stephen de Penchester, being Lord Warden of the Cinque Ports. The next owner, wealthy wool-merchant and four times Mayor of London, Sir John de Pulteney, built the medieval manor house, which includes the famous Great Hall, in about 1340. The fourteenth century house stands complete except for the kitchens, and so remains much as when he lived at Penshurst and, as Shears says "when the Black Prince and his wife Joan the Fair Maid of Kent, were entertained there." Successive owners

Haxted Watermill Museum. *Clive Lawford*

added extensions as the times and contemporary tastes dictated. Many were prominent in service to Crown and State, Sir John Devereux, owner at the turn of the fourteenth century and Lord Warden of the Cinque Ports, added a curtain wall and eight towers to resist any possible invasion from France.

Next Penshurst passed by purchase to Henry V's brother John of Bedford, then to his brother Humphrey, Duke of Gloucester. During the troubled years of the Wars of the Roses in the fifteenth century the house was in the hands of the Dukes of Buckingham, coming, like Hever only fifteen years earlier, into the possession of Henry VIII after the third Duke fell from power and was beheaded. Here that formidable monarch strode the rooms accompanied by Wolsey, his friend and confidant, perhaps also on occasion by Sir William Sidney who had commanded the English at the victorious battle of Flodden Field in 1513 and who had also been at the "Field of the Cloth of Gold". This was the Sir William to whom the boy King Edward VI granted the manor in 1552. The King two years later died in the arms of Sir William's son, Sir Henry who, under Queen Elizabeth, became Lord Deputy in Ireland as well as Lord Warden of the Marches of Wales. It was he who added the north and west fronts.

The River Eden crossed at Edenbridge. *Clive Lawford*

It was his son, Sir Philip, the most famous of the Sidneys (the "god-like Sidney" as Ben Jonson described him) who became poet and courtier, soldier and diplomat, sometimes gaining, sometimes losing favour with Elizabeth. He died in October 1586 as the result of wounds received at the battle of Zutphen in the Netherlands, fighting the Spaniards, by the manner of his death achieving immortal fame. He wove his poetic spell around the formal terraced gardens of Penshurst which had been begun in 1560 and which in the next century were described by Ben Jonson. Philip's younger brother, Robert Sidney, served Queen Elizabeth as Governor of Flushing in the Netherlands, remaining in that office under King James I who later created him Earl of Leicester. The King visited him at Penshurst Place, as Ben Jonson records.

It might have been thought that members of such an eminent family, serving the Crown generation by generation, would be found on the Royalist side in the Civil War, but Philip, Lord Lisle, who became third Earl of Leicester and owner of Penshurst in 1677, had earlier joined the Parliamentary forces with his younger brother, Colonel Algernon Sidney. The latter remained a convinced republican and died on the scaffold in 1683. Loyalties were divided for his sister Dorothy lost her husband, Lord Sunderland, fighting for the King at the battle of Newbury in 1642. His brother Henry, late born, followed the Whig tradition and was one of six conspirators who brought over William III to replace the Stuart James II on the throne of England.

In the eighteenth century, the last Earl of Leicester dying childless, the Penshurst Estate passed twice through the female line. It fell to John Shelley, uncle of the poet Percy Bysshe Shelley, who inherited from his grandmother Elizabeth, surviving daughter of Thomas Sidney, youngest son of the fourth Earl. John Shelley assumed by deed his grandmother's name and arms and became in due course Sir John Shelley Sidney, Baronet. His son Philip was raised to the peerage as Lord De L'Isle and Dudley. The present owner, the Lord De L'Isle and Dudley and first Viscount De L'Isle, is his great-grandson. He has continued the work of restoring the house and gardens which suffered greatly from family divisions and lawsuits in the eighteenth century. It has taken more than a hundred and fifty years to repair the damage of a generation or so of neglect.

Each aspect of the house offers a different perspective. Its plan follows the complicated pattern laid down in the first half century of its existence, its gothic outline masking the simplicity of the original concept of a defended manor house. A sense of continuity is implicit in its style and texture. Its ownership reflects continuing service to the State. The present owner, Viscount De L'Isle, was awarded the V.C. during the Italian campaign of the Allied Armies in the Second World War. He was an M.P. and later Secretary of State for Air under Sir Winston Churchill. He also served as Governor-General of Australia between 1961 and 1964.

CHAPTER THREE

The Town of Five Streams

HOW ASTONISHING to have coal selling at just about a shilling (5p.) per hundredweight; but that was approximately the figure when the Medway Navigation Company brought its first load of coal up to Tonbridge in 1741. Twenty-seven shillings (£1.35) a chaldron (25½ cwt) was the price charged when collecting from the town wharf and, apart from the natural interest of the townspeople in this new venture of transporting heavy goods by water, the attractive price brought plenty of customers to the scene with carts and wagons of every description. Prior to this the idea of using the Medway had been considered on several occasions, especially after Charles II's exile in Holland when he had seen the skill with which the Dutch used their water-ways for transport when the roads in their country were so poor. But not until 1740 had an Act been passed through Parliament to direct that the Medway be made navigable as was stated "From Forest Row in Sussex to Mistress Edmund's wharf in Maidstone."

The upper part of the navigation became the focus for the attentions of a remarkable entrepreneur as will be seen later, the curious grassy ditch on the western outskirts of Tonbridge known as "the straight mile" being the main surviving evidence of his endeavours; but the stretch between Tonbridge and Maidstone became extensively used.

One reason for this interest in transport by water, which seems rather difficult to appreciate in modern times, is the extraordinary way in which the road system of Kent developed in the early days.

Before the Romans came, most of the Belgic settlements were along the lines of the rivers and there have been quite a number of finds of that period along the Medway. These Early Iron Age people then found themselves threatened by a later group who came across from the Continent somewhere between 300 and 200 B.C. and it was as a safeguard against these people that the hill-top forts were normally constructed. Castle Hill near Tonbridge is the site of one of these; or rather, it was thought to be one, but later investigation showed two distinct sets of fortifications dated according to J. H. Money (*Arch. Cant XCI*) c.315 B.C. and c.228 B.C. (This Castle Hill is, of course, quite distinct from the better known Norman castle of Tonbridge). They would protect the early trackway along the Tonbridge-Pembury ridge and also command the crossing of the Medway at Tonbridge by what was later one of

Tonbridge—the Great Bridge built in 1775-6 to replace early narrow bridge.
Kent County Library

the Roman roads into the Weald mentioned by I. D. Margary, but was undoubtedly on the line of an earlier pre-Roman track.

After the Romans left and the land became settled by the Jutes with their less rigid organisation, the county of Kent was divided up into lathes which in turn were subdivided into the Royal estates and the lands held by the free Ceorls. The centre of the latter was a Royal vill and the royal lands were partly for the king's use, partly let out to tenants. All the remainder of the lathe consisted of the ceorls' holdings. This free and easy arrangement was referred to by Lambarde when he said that nowhere were the yeomen "more free and jolly" than in Kent.

In due course of time Manors and Hundreds became the more normal divisions; and the unique "Sulung"—an area that could be ploughed by a team of eight oxen—was still adopted for assessing taxation. But the main feature of all this land tenure was that each lathe had its corresponding "dens" in the Wealden area, so that there would be annual migrations of herds of animals with drovers down to the woods by the old traditional tracks or droves for pasturage—and then a return some seven or eight weeks later, the animals spreading out in various directions when on the flat and more open land to avoid muddy places, thus making the trackway wider and wider. Because the centres of the lathes were in the north of the Medway Gap area and the dens in the Weald, the tracks tended to run north and south; there were practically no roads or tracks heading east to west. Even today the map shows relatively few what might be called "horizontal" roads, and most of these are of fairly modern date; so the value of the Medway navigation in a roughly west-east direction may easily be imagined. The whole of this early development of the manorial system, the dens and the droves is a fascinating study, details of which are most interestingly expounded by K. P. Witney in his book *The Jutish Forest*.

Tonbridge with its crossing of the Medway was a vital point on the route between Hastings, Rye, Winchelsea and London after the Norman Conquest, so naturally King William entrusted it and the safety of the crossing to one of his most loyal supporters, Richard de Clere. There beside the main branch of the Medway, for it separates into five streams here, a motte or mound and a wooden palisaded bailey or court were hurriedly thrown up; and from that time till 1314 the same family held the crossing. To judge from the meticulous notes made by Mr S. Simmons, this trust was no sinecure for first Gilbert de Clare held the place on behalf of Robert of Normandy at the time when Rufus became King William II, so the town, what there was of it, was fired and destroyed. A later Gilbert held the castle on behalf of Matilda (daughter of Henry I) in 1139 but Stephen captured it; later still it was captured by King John's men at the time of Magna Carta, (1215).

All this while the castle defences were being strengthened, the stone keep was erected in 1139, the stone battlements added some thirty-three years later but not till the years of the Barons' War (1264-65) were the gate-houses, drawbridge and barbican added. These final works were of great strength involving two portcullises and three rows of machicolations from which the defenders above could pour boiling oil, molten lead or other suitable material on the heads of attackers to dissuade them.

The close links with the monarchs of the time already noted in connection with Hever and Penshurst, applied here also; in 1272 yet a fourth Gilbert at once swore allegiance to the young Edward I who, at the time of his father's death, was crusading in Palestine; and the King and his Queen, Eleanor, were entertained here before their coronation. On a grimmer note, during the sixteenth century the castle came into the hands of that Dudley, first Duke of Northumberland, whose attempt to make Lady Jane Grey Queen of England failed; and the castle passed to Mary, the rightful Queen. A few years later Elizabeth granted it to her cousin Henry Carew. However that was the high peak of the castle's importance. Like so many others it was "slighted" on Cromwell's orders during the Civil War, succeeding owners used it as a convenient source of building materials. And not until the Urban District Council purchased it in 1900 was any effort made to preserve this historic site. The formal opening of the castle grounds took place on 23rd May, 1900, as was stated "the Wednesday nearest to Queen Victoria's birthday", so now the gatehouse, the only surviving portion, gazes impassively across the lawns at the sliding waters of the river.

Apart from its importance as a river crossing Tonbridge remained what an old guide book referred to as a quiet market town—Elizabeth I granted a market in 1572—with one main street; though the "quietness" in this case included the burning of a Protestant martyr at the stake in the Marian persecution! C. W. Chalklin suggests in *A Kentish Wealden Parish* that the sixteenth century population was between five and six hundred people, absolutely tiny by modern standards.

The Wealden cloth industry which had started in Edward III's reign had reached its peak in about the sixteenth century, and both this and the iron-workings needed water, both for cleansing and for power. There was a fulling mill at Tonbridge, but later cloth was sent to Maidstone for this cleansing and whitening process, while the cutlers of the town were well-known for their fine knives; there were two forges there. These industries, a moderate amount of milling of corn, and its position as the market centre for neighbouring hamlets brought some prosperity to the place, though it is recorded that in 1664 51 per cent of the population were on subsistence level or below, having personal estates of under £10 in value.

Floods in Tonbridge High Street looking south, September 1968. These floods were so serious that Teston Bridge, eleven miles downstream, was almost completely submerged.
Kent and Sussex Courier photograph

Town Quay, Tonbridge. *Tonbridge Historical Society*

Here also the Medway separated into five streams which have, through the years, had a great influence on the town. The main stream near the Castle was crossed by the Great Bridge, three single-arched bridges spanned smaller off-shoots of the river within a matter of thirty yards, and the fifth bridge which had two arches was some little distance to the south, crossing the other important stream of the Medway. In wet weather all the land between these streams was menaced by flooding, and even in comparatively modern times, although the smaller arms are carried beneath the High Street in pipes, the flooding danger occasionally rears its ugly head, as in 1880, 1881, 1891, 1899, 1900, and in 1927 when there were serious floods in the High Street, also in 1968. However flooded meadows were not always such a trial especially when frost was severe, for in 1880 there was much skating on the river, and again between 6th January and 6th March 1893 when the whole of the frozen fields rang with the sound of skates, the scene like a painting of the Flemish school. Many are the stories of the more notable floods as when a habitué of the *Bull* swam out of the window and along the High Street to the *Angel* for his next pint! Alas, the two hostelries concerned are now covered by a supermarket.

One other building in the town was of importance in the early days, the Augustinian Priory of St Mary Magdalene, situated where the railway goods yard is now and founded by Richard de Clere some time in the twelfth century. The Prior and Canons Regular undoubtedly won the trust and confidence of the local populace for when that mighty prelate Cardinal Wolsey began his grandiose schemes of building—not only palaces such Hampton Court but also centres of learning—and sought to sequester the

Priory lands for that purpose there was popular outcry. All the possessions were transferred to Cardinal's College, Oxford, later called Christ Church.

It was probably because of this that a local merchant, Sir Andrew Judd, conceived the idea of founding a free grammar school, which became Tonbridge School. In his early years he had been apprenticed to the Skinners Company, and became a merchant of Muscovy making expeditions to Russia, the Volga and Astrakhan. This energetic and far-sighted man who was Lord Mayor of London in 1530 and six times Master of the Skinners Company, realised the need to endow his school and arrange for its administration and financing after his death; he entrusted the governorship to his City Livery Company, (as is still the case today), with property in the region of St Pancras in London to provide funds. The Medway, of course, has always been of inestimable advantage to the school, and certainly over the last hundred years has been used for boating and swimming, including the training of the school rowing Fours and Eights.

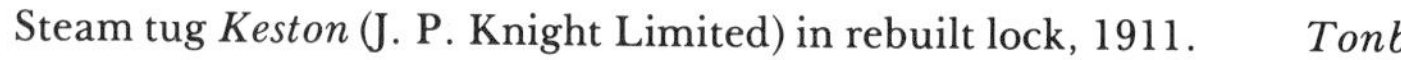

Steam tug *Keston* (J. P. Knight Limited) in rebuilt lock, 1911. *Tonbridge Historical Society*

So even in the sixteenth and seventeenth centuries the river was of considerable importance to the town; but then came a time when its development was the direct cause of a great surge of prosperity, leading to a period of growth which has continued in one way or another to the present day.

At the beginning of this chapter reference was made to the first load of coal brought up by the "Company of Proprietors of the Navigation of the River Medway", to give them their full title. Once the Act of 1740 had been passed through Parliament the Company began to press ahead with their plans with commendable speed, being helped by several important promoters, chief among whom was Lionel, Duke of Dorset, who was Chairman of the Directors for many years. The need for such a waterway was very apparent at that time of uncertainty, with wars in Europe leading shortly to actions against the French both in Canada and India. There were great quantities of English oak in the Weald, the most suitable wood of all for use in building warships in the Royal dockyard at Chatham. The river was a splendid way of transporting it without the hindrance of the appalling roads.

Another interesting result of the canal was that houses in Tonbridge began to be built in brick. Up till this time all buildings had been faced with weather-boarding owing to the difficulty of conveying lime from the nearest

Sprits'l barge *Kingfisher*, with all gear lowered in tow of steam tug *Keston*, swinging round a narrow bend. *Tonbridge Historical Society*

sources, either Wrotham Hill or the Maidstone area. Now this new route opened up wonderful possibilities and people started to work the brick-clay in the neighbourhood, the Canal Company even putting up a lime kiln not far away from the Town Wharf, as A. H. Neve mentions in his *Tonbridge of Yesterday*.

However, all was not easy for the promoters as they were up against the very difficulties that had deterred earlier innovators, the awkward fact that there is a drop of 56 feet in levels from Tonbridge to Maidstone which necessitates locks. Also there was the problem of weirs as the riparian landowners used such means both to indicate their boundaries and also to create suitable pools for the taking of eels and fish of all kinds. Yet a third obstacle was provided by the mills both in Tonbridge and downstream which required a good head of water for their mill-pools. Lastly there were the famous medieval bridges with their restricted head-room.

Despite all these snags and the fact that they were very short of capital the Canal Company very soon started to build up their own fleet of barges and began trading as coal merchants, supplying among others the town gas-works in the early years of the nineteenth century. These works were built right alongside the river having their own wharf to facilitate the unloading of coal supplies; and even at the beginning of this century when electricity was coming into prominence, the electricity works were sited near the river with a special branch canal for the fuel supply. Agricultural products of all kinds were handled, there were regular traffic jams of carts bringing flour from Watts Cross mill to the Town Quay for shipment down to Maidstone, hops, of course, also featured; and cargoes such as lime, stone and gravel were brought up, as well as coal. In the early days the barges were hauled along by men with tow-ropes—tracking as it was called; later horses towed the barges. Both these activities would need a well made and well maintained towpath which nowadays provides an excellent riverside walk, a convenient perch for anglers and a mooring place for boats and pleasure craft.

It is worth remembering that just about the time that the Canal Company was starting its operations the turnpike movement was bringing at least some improvement to the major roads although the minor ones were still, of course, the responsibility of the parish; the road from Sevenoaks to Tonbridge and on to Tunbridge Wells was one of the earliest of these turnpike roads. This meant more travellers passing through the town, more chances of trade for inns; and, as soon as stage coaches began to ply, a good centre for exchanging horses. Hence the two new activities together brought increasing prosperity and by about 1780 Tonbridge was an important trading centre.

The Canal Company, however, was soon up against opposition. Law suits seemed to occur with alarming regularity. They had to fight a case brought by the owner of Branbridge's mill in connection with water rights; fortunately

East Lock, Lock Number 4, showing typical river scenery.
Kent and Sussex Courier photograph

through marriage to the boss's daughter, this particular mill passed into the hands of an owner more favourable to the Company so there was no further trouble on that score, as we shall see later. But in the 1820s, by which time the Company had become a profitable undertaking, an entrepreneur of the name of Christie bought the town mill from the previous owners, along with all water-rights etc. and, with some other colleagues formed what was called the Penshurst Company with the idea of extending the navigation upstream. This of course was very dangerous for the water reserves of the original Canal Company who were down stream of him and relied on the river flow to operate their locks. They realised it and obtained an injunction, at considerable cost, preventing him from interfering with their water; but he at once reacted by diverting water through a new cut near the waterworks. There were fights between Christie's navvies and Canal Company men, barges at the Town Wharf were occasionally stranded without water, he even initiated court cases alleging interference with his water-rights at his mill. Finally, possibly over-playing his hand, he sought to promote a Bill in Parliament to give him control over the Canal Company's affairs. But the expenses he had incurred in pursuing what seemed very like a vendetta against the Company now caught up with him. The Bill was thrown out, he became bankrupt and promptly left the country in haste, bound for America.

Now a new trouble loomed, the Bill allowing the South Eastern Railway Company to construct a line from Redhill through Tonbridge, down to Ashford and on to Folkestone and Dover. The Canal Company realised the danger and put a steam tug on the river to speed up their own transport, but a further Paddock Wood-Maidstone rail link began to affect their trade. A further court case about a road at Yalding went against them, they had a case of embezzlement among their own employees, and sadly went into receivership having done so much to improve the prosperity of Tonbridge and the sensible use of the river. A new Medway Lighterage Company was formed handling some 10,000 tons of coal, timber, stone and building materal per annum, and the steam tug *Tonbridge Castle* was put on the river by Knight's of Rochester; but the deterioration and ultimate collapse of the lock at East Farleigh finished that endeavour. Now modern water authorities maintain the locks and the river in its most charming stretches but purely as a water resource and for recreational purposes; and the limpid eddies slide peacefully past the fisherman as he casts, the locks handle motor boats and small sailing craft, the ancient bridges watch serenely over the summer holiday-makers. The dream of the "Grand Southern Canal", surveyed in 1803 which would have linked Tonbridge with Portsmouth in the west as well as with Maidstone and the Thames via the Higham Canal to the east, is but a faint memory.

How foolish it is today that, in our misguided desire for speed, we make so little use of all available waterways for moving heavier and imperishable goods and thus relieve our over-strained roads. But so much of the prosperity of modern Tonbridge, with its printing works, its unique hand-made bricks, the old-established sports goods manufacturers—so typical of the county where even today many of the villages boast at least one cricket team—is a reminder of the profound influence of our river upon its fortunes. It would be invidious to attempt to detail the many companies connected with the town, but there is this special link with the county's favourite game. The Duke family started their cricket ball manufacture as long ago as 1760 near Penshurst, then moving in 1841 to Chiddingstone Causeway, as mentioned earlier. By the end of the nineteenth century as is noted by Barty-King in his *Quiltwinders and Pod Shavers*, Wisden's and Thomas Ives were in competition in Tonbridge with the Kent Cricket and Football Company owned by Dukes; these later amalgamated into the Tonbridge Sports Industries. How reassuring it is that the Duke family firm still continues with its skilled craft at Chiddingstone Causeway. Because of the importance of water in the provision of power for the early mills, mention must also be made of the Ramhurst Mill, an old corn-mill, at Leigh just above Tonbridge. This was adapted for the milling of gunpowder as a result of the scientific experiments of Sir Humphry Davy, better known for his development of the Miners' Safety Lamp, and his partnership with the local banker George Children. The latter had a keen interest in science and was one of the earliest to experiment with electric storage batteries at his fine Georgian mansion Ferox Hall, adjacent to which he built a laboratory. So not only has the river contributed to Tonbridge's prosperity but it was also known and enjoyed by inventors of the calibre of Davy and Children whose work has been of such influence on life right up to the present day.

CHAPTER FOUR

Tributaries at Twyford and Yalding

THERE IS a great contrast between the Medway Canal Company barges full of coal or lime being towed laboriously up or down stream in the nineteenth century and the scene on the river today. Ten hours was reckoned to be the time for the journey from Tonbridge to Maidstone, a little longer on the way upstream. Usually the barges were those of the Canal Company, but sometimes a big spritsail barge could be seen, with all her masts and gear lowered because of the low bridges. These craft, symbols of industry and enterprise would go gliding along at the end of a tow-rope, drawn at about two miles an hour by one horse, through the most peaceful and rural scenery—hop gardens and orchards white with blossom.

Nowadays the river below Tonbridge teems with boats in summer but these are purely pleasure craft. Sadly the punts and small rowing boats have been largely superseded by motorised craft some of which, with powerful engines, carve their rapid way to the distress of anglers, peril to other river users and damage to the banks. However, to be fair, it is only a very few boat-owners who do not observe the speed regulations and thus spoil the enjoyment of others. Many small sailing-dinghies slide more peacefully beside the grassy banks, the windings of the river providing plenty of practice in tacking, although watch has to be kept on the headroom under the bridges which is usually just enough and no more! However, on a sunny day in summer what could be more perfect than to sunbathe like this, on the move?

What changes these waters have seen. In Tonbridge itself there was an old-established firm of boat builders and repairers on New Wharf until the 1950s. More recently a company started to mould fibre-glass hulls, but these are usually taken by road to their fitting-out berths far away. The Fours and Eights of the Tonbridge School Boat Club dip their oars with rhythmic precision in the mile and three quarters down to Eldridge's Lock, the spreading circles from their blades patterning the surface to either side of their seething wake. Astonishing to reflect that the Hammer Dyke which joins the river just below the next lock once provided power for an old iron-forge in the fourteenth century, one of the earliest in Kent.

Hartlake bridge nearby carries the road across from Tudeley Hale to Golden Green, all of this important hop country, also ablaze with the blossom

of many orchards as pear, cherry and apple succeed one another in spring-time. But in these days the tendency is to plant smaller trees which can the more easily be pruned and sprayed and the fruit gathered, and the alluvial soil near the water-meadows is suitable for high density planting. Over all this stretch of country looms the tall grey tower of the weird structure called Hadlow Castle, a folly of turrets, walls and gatehouses amid trees, put up by an eccentric gentleman, Mr Barton May, in 1810.

The river winds on enchantingly, here and there narrowing to a lock, sometimes spreading out or dodging around some great weeping willow, or with side-channels forming a tree-fringed islet. Nearly parallel to its flow a minor road runs some half-mile to the north through hamlets and villages with attractive names Little Mill, Snoll Hatch, East Peckham; and at this last we are close to Branbridges, the cause of much trouble to the Canal Company. The river spreads itself into side-streams and marshes, at Sluice Weir lock a good deal of silting takes place and dredging has to be undertaken each year to keep a depth of four feet. The foot-path at the waterside gives a good access for anglers, several stretches being private but others controlled by various societies such as the Maidstone Victory Angling Society and the Tonbridge Angling Society. And, in this beautiful stretch, with farms, hop-gardens, woods and the picturesque oast-houses, there is also enjoyable fishing for roach, carp, bream, chub and pike among others.

Strange to reflect that in 1751, as Neve tells us, Henry Martyr, the owner of the Branbridges mill brought a successful case against the Canal Company over water-rights as we have seen. He was then followed as proprietor by one of his mill-hands, Thomas Boorman, who had chosen the best of all roads to fortune, marrying the owner's daughter. This man Boorman's nephew purchased sufficient shares in the Canal Company to influence its policy; and for a number of years the company was really managed from Branbridges, the representative at the Tonbridge Town Wharf being merely a manager.

Probably very few of those who steer their boats along this favourite stretch between here and Yalding Lees know much about this former conflict over water-rights. Perhaps they dream of long trips under sail, of taking part in ocean races, of the scend of the great rollers out in the Atlantic and the tearing wind, not realising that Sir Francis Drake, one of the first to sail round the world, learnt his seamanship not so far away in a hoy* down at the Medway mouth. To handle a little dinghy on waters as quiet as these above Yalding still demands concentration and teaches watermanship—and may be the first step to ventures on the great oceans of the world. Very likely also they

◀ Hadlow Castle. *Kent and Sussex Courier photograph*

*Hoy—a small coastal sailing craft of up to about 60 tons.

have little idea of the origins of the two streams that join the river at the aptly named Twyford. Yet both of them, the Teise and the Beult, start their meanderings many miles away, probing the very heart of Kentish country. Although the last-named is the more important tributary, the Teise was notable for the use made of it by the iron-masters of the Weald, use which is proved by the ever-recurring names "Furnace Mill", "Old Forge", "Forge Farm", "Furnace Pond".

It would be impossible to detail all the interesting villages through which this little stream—really not more than a brook in fact—makes its way to join the Medway. Tributaries of even lesser size link up from east and west, it separates itself into two branches not far from Marden Beech, one of them becoming known as the "Twist", a name justly descriptive of its course. As was the case with the headwaters of the Medway proper it is quite a task to puzzle out the springs which feed it. Round about Frant and the Downs south of Tunbridge Wells there is another distinct watershed, the Sussex river Rother linking its youthful waters to the west and the little rivulets of Beult and Teise gathering to the north and east.

Branbridges, six miles downstream from Tonbridge. This picture shows the medieval bridge which was replaced by the present one in 1906. *Kent County Library*

Bowl Bridge Reservoir, forming a 220-acre nature reserve with recreational pursuits included.
Southern Water Authority

Close to Lamberhurst, there has been a great new undertaking, in complete contrast with the old pools intended for making a head of water to power furnace-bellows or forge-hammers, the creation of a glimmering sheet of water by the flooding of three valleys. This Bewl Bridge Reservoir, though it has drowned an attractive little sweep of country, has brought into being a nature reserve of some 220 acres, with the peculiar fascination which all great sweeps of water possess, the reflections of surrounding hills, the ever-changing colours and lights from the clouds above. Here the authorities intend to encourage recreational pursuits; already the reservoir has been stocked with rainbow trout for the benefit of anglers, and birds of the lakes and reed-beds will certainly use this sanctuary, for Canada and Brent Geese already favour these waters with their strange honking calls and the beating of great wings. It is by this same little river Bewl that Scotney Castle stands, the round grey moated tower dating back to the time of Richard II, the stream filling the lily-covered moat. Passing from the Ashburnhams to Henry Chicheley, Archbishop of Canterbury it later came into the hands of the Darell family and more recently the Husseys. Down the same lane, a little further on is the brick-built early eighteenth century house named Finchcocks, with its fine collection of musical instruments of the period.

Over the other side of the Lamberhurst Down, in the direction of Tunbridge Wells, were several forges in the aptly named Furnace Wood; and reaching even further back into history are the ruins of Bayham Abbey, grey and gaunt beside their lake, a house established by the White Canons in 1200. Many other foundations of theirs were in this neighbourhood—at Lamberhurst and Horsmonden among others—but in 1525 Wolsey absorbed these, along with the Priory at Tonbridge; and, on his disgrace and death the lands came into the hands of Henry VIII. From the time of Elizabeth I onward a series of owners ran the forges here until finally the iron-working ceased and the present nineteenth century house was built as the mansion house of the estate.

There is a reminder of something else beside iron-workings, for not far from Hoathly is a sixteenth century timbered cottage known as the Owl House once supposedly used by the "owlers" or wool smugglers of Elizabethan times.

Furnace Mill between Bayham Abbey and Lamberhurst is a reminder of the Gloucester furnace, named after Queen Anne's son, which was in operation under various owners from the sixteenth to the eighteenth centuries, making not only the iron railings for St Paul's Cathedral but also cannon for the Royal Navy—which, like the railings, were shipped down the Medway. There seems to be rather a cloud over the activities of the last owner of this furnace, one Richard Tapsell, as he was suspected of selling his wares, smuggling them out in fact, to the French at the time of considerable tension between our two countries. The Gloucester furnace finally closed down in 1765.

Lamberhurst itself is a typical Wealden village with attractive tiled and weather-boarded cottages on its steep hill. Somehow it is difficult to associate such a very Kentish place, so entirely rural, with the bygone industry of iron-forging.

From here the Teise goes wriggling along the green valley in the direction of Goudhurst and Horsmonden, a meandering streamlet soon coming in to join it from the south-east. This has its source in the area of Bedgbury Forest, still rich in stately trees which are a haze of green in spring, a glorious russet in autumn; but even here close to the wooded glades, Furnace Farm is a reminder of the days of Wealden iron and of the source of some of the wealth that helped to maintain the Bedgbury estate. There is a special Bedgbury chapel in St Mary's Church, Goudhurst, whose massive square sandstone tower on the hill-top can be seen for miles around, and brasses and monuments here tell of the owners, of John Bedgbury the first husband of Anne Roper. On his death in 1424 she married again, this time Walter Culpeper, and this brought the Bedgbury estate into that great Kentish family whose interests covered

Aylesford, East Farleigh and Hollingbourne among other places. They were influential enough to entertain Queen Elizabeth I here for a whole day in 1573 when she was making one of her Royal Progresses about her country.

Till well on in the seventeenth century they held these lands until at length they passed from Thomas Culpeper to a certain enterprising gentleman, by name James Hayes, whom Goodsall mentions as "a very ingenious man" and who is supposed to have used the salvaged proceeds of a Spanish treasure galleon to build the present house.

A later owner was William Carr, Viscount Beresford, one of Wellington's most able commanders during the Peninsular War. His military career was extraordinary for he was at Toulon with Admiral Lord Hood, then took part in the capture of places as far apart as Cape Colony (now Cape of Good Hope) and Buenos Aires, made a daring escape when this latter place was recaptured and was then entrusted with the re-organisation of the army of our allies, the

Hop picking. *South Eastern Newspapers Limited*

Portuguese, in 1809. Assisting to win Busaco, Portugal, in 1810, he commanded our victorious army at Albuera, Spain, took part in the grim storming of Badajoz, and was at the concluding actions of Salamanca and Toulouse. Even then his service to the country was not ended for he was Master of the Ordnance in the Duke of Wellington's administration.

When finally the estate had to be split up, the house became a school while the Forestry Commission assumed responsibility for the woodlands, planting a special pinetum, a nursery for young conifers, in this most suitable spot.

Well downstream from Horsmonden a rivulet joins from roughly a north-westerly direction, flowing down from one of the largest of the lakes formed by damming streamlets to provide a weight of water for operating furnace-bellows. This is the magnificent Horsmonden Furnace Pond, a splendid place for wildfowl and fish, seeming rather remote amid its trees even today. R. H. Goodsall tells us that one of the owners of this furnace, Thomas Browne, was making guns for the Navy in 1589, the year after the Armada. His son John had contracts to make guns for the Army and Navy and later also for Cromwell; and another of the strange iron grave stones or slabs—this one for his wife Martha—is to be found in Horsmonden Church; which Dorothy Gardiner had such difficulty in locating, as told in her entertaining *Companion into Kent*.

Stephen's Bridge, Headcorn, River Beult. The metal ties and sharp-pointed cutwater are typical of local construction. *Author's collection*

Massive stonework in Kentish Rag — the medieval Town Bridge at Yalding, looking up towards the church. *Author's collection*

The number of ancient bridges is a feature of both the Teise and its fellow tributary the Beult, though the latter river has the greater score. Here we are presented with one of those curious contrasts which occur in connection with the tributaries no less than with the parent river the Medway. The mills and ponds along the Teise were principally connected with iron-workings in the middle ages, the ponds and dams along the Beult had more to do with cloth. Both these industries, which led to such considerable prosperity as evidenced by the spaciousness and size of the parish churches, are now but a memory; the ancient bridges with their triangular refuges for pedestrians now mostly carry a relatively small amount of traffic — a very fortunate thing in view of the length and weight of the modern juggernaut!

Vita Sackville-West, who had such a great love for every different season of the year in the countryside, speaks pleasurably of the valleys of the Beult and the Medway in her *Country Notes*. She, in particular, would have known and enjoyed the Kentish rivers as the Hammer stream which joins the Beult not far from Headcorn, runs close by her beloved Sissinghurst Castle. An astonishing number of these historic moated buildings are to be found along the course of the river and its tributary streams. How greatly do the personalitites of the owners influence their mellow stones and brick-work and, of course, at Sissinghurst, the famous gardens as well as the Tudor gate-tower. How great has been the effect on the whole countryside of the aftermath of early wars—from gun-foundries to the Flemish cloth-workers who settled in the Weald during the French wars of Edward III's time, the Huguenots who fled here after the dreadful massacres of 1572 or, in the case of Sissinghurst, the French prisoners of war who wrought such havoc to the house by cutting up doors and bannisters for fire wood.

The medieval bridges along these rivers are closely linked with the growth of the droves referred to in the previous chapter. Several of them are on the sites of fords which were probably approached by causeways in earlier times, for the whole of the area round about the course of the Beult would have become an impassable marsh in wet weather. The land is predominantly flat, with a subsoil of Wealden clay, the river winding gently to and fro, nowadays through farm-land with herds of cattle but in former times much more wooded. Sometimes the banks of the stream near a ford or crossing would be reinforced by a corduroy of logs laid across the track to give some stability to the miry way; sometimes there might be a crude wooden bridge. In due time as parishes became responsible for the roads within their boundaries, it would impose a considerable strain on their resources to maintain a bridge, so frequently there are mentions of legacies in ancient registers for the repair of the bridge.

The Beult really becomes a river at the strangely named Westpherhawk Farm, where some four or so small streams from the Bethersden neighbourhood link up, and from there flows to the delightful weather-boarded village of Smarden. Oast-houses, either still operational or else converted into dwellings become increasingly a feature of this very Kentish countryside, and Smarden itself is most attractive. Although frequently among the leaders in the Kent's Best-Kept Village Competitions it is really a small town steeped in history—it was granted a market as long ago as the reign of Edward III. Most unusual is the approach to St Michael's Church where the medieval weather-boarded houses crouch close together on either side of the road, and the actual entrance to the church is by way of a passage beneath the upper storey of one of them. The fourteenth century church, too, is unusual, the wide nave being entirely without side aisles, thus giving a great impression of spaciousness. The old town bridge across the Beult, undoubtedly on the site of some earlier crossing, is typical with a sharp cut-water on the up-river side of the central pier to lessen resistance in times of severe flooding.

Headcorn, too, has the ancient Stephen's Bridge, locally known as the Bishops's Bridge, where the cut-water comes up to the parapet making a little

V-shaped refuge for pedestrians. This again is a typical feature of these medieval structures when the road width was no more than eleven or twelve feet. In the great days of the Kentish broad-cloth, there must have been plenty of coming and going across this bridge for Headcorn was an important centre of the cloth-trade, the fine old cloth-hall known as Shakespeare House still standing in the High Street. Also lands and manors belonging to the Archbishop of Canterbury stretched well south into the Weald, West Kent and Sussex so this particular crossing of the Beult would have been especially important. Here, too, the great family of Culpeper was an influence for the church of St Peter and St Paul owed its building to them, and is a fine example of construction in Kentish ragstone.

About 1½ miles downstream from Headcorn, another stream, the Sherway, joins and the river assumes an ever more important guise as it weaves to and fro presently crossing what was formerly a Roman road between Staplehurst and Sutton Valence. The Hawkenbury bridge which carries the road is one of the longest and is a modern structure, but Goodsall mentions that the original stone structure can be seen further upstream.

While on the subject of the importance of the Wealden cloth industry it is interesting to note that, as it declined and the centre of the trade moved north in the days of Cromwell, a certain amount of flax-growing was substituted in the Smarden and Headcorn areas and the manufacture of linen cloth was encouraged. However by the eighteenth century the industry was dead, the mills abandoned and very few traces of them remain, except for the mill-pools and leats which provide good sport for anglers.

The charming village of Sutton Valence, too, owes its famous school to the cloth industry. Just as was the case with Sir Andrew Judd at Tonbridge, a Livery man of one of the City Livery Companies—in this instance the Cloth-Workers Company—one William Lambe, founded it in 1575; and the school and many of the houses in the village were appropriately built in local Kentish ragstone.

Along a minor road from Chart Sutton there is another old bridge very possibly dating from the fifteenth century, locally known as Hazel Bridge, according to Coles Finch in his *Medway River and Valley*. It is really an elongated causeway crossing over two channels of the river.

A little further downstream the Twist joins, the Beult winds on through more orchard country, coming to weirs and at length to the ancient little market town of Yalding which it enters beneath the fifteenth century Town Bridge. Only a very short distance up the main channel of the Medway the Teise has added its strength to the flow passing beneath the lovely medieval Twyford Bridge; so now the river, united with its major tributaries, starts its loop through the hop country on its way to Maidstone.

CHAPTER FIVE

"The Finest Seven Miles . . . "

THE CANAL Company comes in to the picture yet again for when they were granted their right of navigation they decided to make a cut, slicing off the whole of the Yalding bend, and construct the Hampstead Lane lock. This was an undoubted advantage for their barges and has had the excellent result of making the stretch between Twyford Bridge and Yalding a splendid quiet backwater for boats, anglers and picnic parties.

Just below Twyford Bridge which has no less than four arches with pointed cut-waters and is one of the most interesting of all the medieval bridges on the river, is the wide stretch of meadow known as Yalding Lees. In former times this was a cricket field, for Yalding always fielded two teams and still has a Saturday and a Sunday team, but now the Lees is used as a car park for the anglers, swimmers and others wishing to use this peaceful backwater.

The Canal Company's short cut, the Hampstead Lane Canal as it was called, was yet another item that caused controversy and, in the end, legal action. Running alongside it from Yalding Station through to the Lees was the actual "Hampstead Lane" and, having embanked the new canal and therefore secured the foundations of the lane, the Company duly surfaced it in accordance with an agreement to maintain it "in perpetuity". But when County Councils were established, with responsibility for highways, the Company was advised that they need no longer accept responsibility. Unfortunately as neither the Company nor the Council did anything about it the lane became full of pot-holes and finally a case was brought against the Canal Company. Under a settlement negotiated with the Maidstone Urban District Council, the Company offered to pay £350 for the Council to take over liability for the lane and a further £150 for the bridge. This dispute contributed to the final winding up of the concern in 1911.

Yalding, as already mentioned in the previous chapter, is of ancient origin, very probably going back to Saxon times. Certainly the fine old church of St Peter and St Paul is basically of thirteenth century work, though the side-aisles were widened in the fourteenth century and the wagon roof of the nave dates from the fifteenth or early sixteenth. The old stone tower is interesting in that the lower portion dates back to before the Norman Conquest, it has a side spiral staircase topped with an Elizabethan onion-shaped dome, and most of the fine peal of bells date back to 1696. The wide-spreading water-meadows close to Twyford bridge were always subject to much flooding at the junction of the Teise with the Medway so this is the probable reason for the early settlement at Yalding which is slightly higher; though here again, with the Beult running in, there was some danger of flooding at the lower end of what John Ireland (in Henry VIII's time) called "a prety townlet".

The Town Bridge of Yalding is of fifteenth century work, though in an excavation in 1969 foundations were discovered going back to the thirteenth century and large timber beams that suggested an even earlier bridge of wood. It is the largest medieval bridge in Kent (450 feet) and in the local guide-book on Yalding Mr John Parsons mentions that it is really two bridges side by side, the addition to accommodate extra traffic; he refers, too, to the "Hospitarii Pontifices", a band of bridge-builders connected with the monks of Rochester who are thought to have built all the early Medway bridges.

As with Judd at Tonbridge and Lambe at Sutton Valence, a native of Yalding who had been in business in London as a Haberdasher determined to found a free grammar school. This successful trader, William Cleaves, provided in his will £100 for the building, and a 48 acre farm as endowment; Cleaves Grammar School flourished from 1663 until 1921 having among its pupils the poet Edmund Blunden who made many references to his home town in his poems. Cleaves House, as it is now called, still stands, timber-framed and tile-hung. Outside it, on the village green is the 1786 lock-up, the "Cage" as it was known, with its iron-studded door and grille. There are a number of

The quiet backwater of Yalding Marina. *Kent and Sussex Courier photograph*

interesting and attractive houses and cottages down the High Street, many of them weather-boarded and most dating back at least to the eighteenth century, some even earlier. The fine Queen Anne house known as Court Lodge, and the Georgian Warde's Moat, formerly the Vicarage, are particularly noteworthy; but unhappily the famous "High Houses" mentioned by so many early writers and described by Sir Charles Igglesden in his *Saunter through Kent* are no more; they were demolished as unsafe in 1938. However they were of very unusual appearance, timber-framed, with plaster work and weather-boarding on the strange overhanging storeys.

Behind the site of these High Houses there used to be a ford and also a wharf, though this was not the one used for the trans-shipment of the iron goods from the Weald into barges that would take them down to Maidstone or to the Royal Navy dockyard at Chatham. That was close to the present Hampstead Lock near the downstream end of the loop of the Medway that passes close to the village. It is extraordinary, looking at the gleaming white motor-cruisers and the dinghies with their coloured hulls and sails to think that as long ago as three hundred years this very same river used to shift such war-like articles as cannon which had been cast miles away in the furnaces of the Weald.

The other important activity that has long been associated with Yalding is the growing of hops; here again we have a close link with the cloth industry as it was the Flemish weavers during Edward III's reign who introduced the use of

Yalding High Street, looking towards the church. *Author's collection*

Hop picking in the old style. *South Eastern Newspapers Limited*

hops into this country. At first they used to import hops that had been grown and dried in the Low Countries; these were for flavouring and preserving beer. In due time hop-growing came across the channel when popular demand for beer as opposed to ale increased; by about the fifteenth or sixteenth century Flemish growers had come over here to teach the farmers, in the cloth-making area of Kent in particular, the details of growing and processing the crop. In a most informative article on oasts Anthony Cronk in *Archaeologia Cantiana 1978* mentions Reynolde Scot of Smeeth who produced the first English book on hop-culture in 1574 with full instructions as to how a grower should provide himself with a suitable drying-kiln or "Oste". Initially barns were adapted with drying-floor and fireplace beneath, most farmers having a small hop-garden as well as other crops and hence making use of such facilities as were already to hand to dry the hops. However by the eighteenth century there was greatly increased production and the tall cone-shaped buildings which are such a feature of the Kentish scene were developed, the white cowl on top being swung away from the wind and thus creating suction to draw the hot air through the hops. These oast-houses are especially common all along this Medway valley, for the alluvial soil on top of brick earth is ideal for hop-culture: this area has been the centre of cultivation at least since Daniel Defoe mentioned in 1724 "that it was around Maidstone that hops were first planted in this country in any quantity." This particular association with Kent is the reason why the prancing horse symbol of the county was stencilled on so many of the hop-pockets, those tall attractive sacks containing 168 pounds of hops, to be found in breweries all up and down the country.

So it is that over the years there has been a great influx of pickers into Yalding at the time of the hop-harvest, whole families from East London swarming down here year after year to dwell in the hoppers' huts that can still be seen and gypsies, too, congregated with their gay caravans. Today, though the hop-bines are cut and hauled away by tractors to the oasts behind the High Street where machinery strips the hops, it is still necessary to employ a certain number of pickers who pitch their ultra modern caravans in the little un-surfaced track near the old ford of the Beult; the scent of hops wafts over the village in the still evening air as of old.

Only a matter of a mile or so away, on the hillside on the opposite side of the valley, is Nettlestead which had the usual medieval arrangement of manor house and church in close proximity to each other, the barns and buildings connected with Nettlestead Court grey stone and tiled, the church unique because of the unexpectedly tall and graceful windows in a comparatively small parish church. It has a strange little thirteenth century tower seemingly hunched into its shoulders; but shortly after this tower was added to the building it appears that the existing nave and chancel were taken down and the present ones erected in their place, not a usual kind of alteration except when a church has needed additional side-aisles because of a vastly enlarged congregation. Nothing of the sort was the case here, however, and it was thought that the re-building, carried out at the expense and on the orders of the Lord of the Manor, Reginald de Pympe, who had already reconstructed Nettlestead Court, was entirely to incorporate the unique windows. These were fitted with very lovely fifteenth century glass—though of course much of it displaced and weathered—particularly showing the heraldic shields of the many families with whom the de Pympes were linked by marriage. The same family owned Pimp's at East Farleigh.

They were a Norman family originally, holding the Manor from the de Cleres of Tonbridge and later from the de Staffords. With the great increase in trade with the continent during the time of Edward III and afterwards, the de Pympes prospered, becoming people of much importance in the county, several members of the family being appointed Sheriffs of Kent. Later, after the turmoil of the Wars of the Roses had ceased, another Sir Reginald served King Henry VII in Ireland under Sir Edward Poynings; this was an extra-

The medieval bridge at Teston, with the church and Barham Court in the distance.
Kent County Library

ordinary position for him as he had been implicated in the Duke of Buckingham's rebellion in 1483—of which mention will be made later—but it may be ascribed to his family connection with Poynings. Sir Edward married the daughter of a Sir John Scott and her brother married Sir Reginald Pympe's daughter.

In 1823 William Cobbett wrote about this part of the river—as quoted by Joan Severn in her *Teston Story*, "From Maidstone to this place (Meryworth) is about 7 miles, and these are the finest 7 miles that I have ever seen in England or anywhere else." In view of this reference it would seem right to take a look at Mereworth and the great woodland on the ridge to the north of it. The village itself has a few eighteenth century houses and cottages but the chief interest of the place is Mereworth Castle, built between 1720 and 1730 on the site of an earlier castle. It seems extraordinary to see this copy of Palladio's* Villa Capra at Vicenza set amid wide-spreading gardens and park-land, its great central dome and porticos on either side with their Ionic columns in strange contrast with the very English scenery around. It is interesting that this and Chiswick House are the only two copies of the Villa Capra still in existence.

*Italian architect (1508-80) who revived Classical Roman styles and influenced English architects to form a Palladian school.

Moving on from Nettlestead, surrounded by orchards and hop-gardens the Medway now sweeps round to Wateringbury, then wriggles its way down towards Teston Lock, getting deeper and wider in this most beautiful reach. At Wateringbury Bridge the road and railway station close at hand make access to the river easy for holiday-makers, anglers and family parties, there is a water-mill and the Church of St John the Baptist, to quote an old guide book, "has interesting features". Apart from the fourteenth century porch, these must surely include the strange dark oaken staff which is preserved inside the church and which is known by the curious name of the Dumb Bors-holder of Chart. Equipped with chain and spike it dates back very possibly to before the Norman Conquest, the name being derived from a Saxon root, and was mentioned by Hasted as an early form of the maintenance of good behaviour. Being only a spiked stick it is obviously "dumb" and has to be deputised for by parish officers. Also in this church is the very fine Style memorial, dating from 1628, Sir Oliver Style having been a Sheriff of London.

As the Medway slides towards Teston Lock, tall trees on the one hand, the tow path and bushes on the other, the ruins of the old Tutsham Mill appear, which was burned down in 1885. This was a linseed and cattle cake mill, an old established concern as there had been reference to a mill at Teston as far back as 1745. From here with the lush grass of the meadows all around, another medieval bridge comes into sight. This, the Teston Bridge, originally had seven arches but some repair and alteration to the central arch in the eighteenth century took place to make it more easily navigable for the barges of the Canal Company and later re-building in 1820 cut the number of arches down to six of which three are actually over the river. It is a lovely bridge, of much the same date as those at Twyford and Yalding, the roadway only some ten or eleven feet wide and the cut-waters above the massive piers providing the typical triangular refuges for foot passengers. As has been mentioned in Chapter One the river valley has always been liable to flooding and in spite of much admirable work by the Kent River Board, now merged into the Southern Water Authority, this problem still persists. Yet this old rag-stone bridge, massive and picturesque still leads modern motors across the Medway and allows motor-cruisers to pass beneath, but it has additional iron ties, visible here and there, to provide extra strength. And strength it certainly needs for the flood waters fill the valley just here after severe rainfall and occasionally the parapet of the bridge is only just visible above the hurrying foam.

In her interesting little book Joan Severn refers to a well-known local water diviner, George Latter, who died in 1960 and who always asserted that there

West Farleigh, a typical Kentish church. *Author's collection* ▶

was a "buried channel" below the present bed of the river at this point, and that there were many underground streams, in the valley. All this links up with the discoveries made further downstream in the Medway Gap, which were referred to in Chapter One.

The village itself, on the rising ground to the north of the Medway, goes far back into history, very probably as far as the Belgic pre-Roman times; certainly there was a Roman villa just at the top of the slope up from the river. Unfortunately information available is not sufficiently detailed to show how large this villa was. Nor does there seem to be sufficient evidence to establish a suggested Roman crossing of the river, though there were originally fords here, at Nettlestead and near the bridge at Barming. Clearly, though, there was a little community here in Jutish times for even before the Norman Conquest the people of Teston were scheduled among those responsible for the planking and maintenance of one of the piers of Rochester bridge.

After William I had established Norman control of the land, he granted Teston to his rapacious half-brother Odo of Bayeux who seems to have held vast estates in Kent. However, within a relatively short time, the usual rivalries and jealousies had developed and the lands reverted to the Crown, though the tenant throughout was the same Robert de Crèvecoeur who had so much to do with Leeds, Kent. The confusions of the Barons War led to Royal occupation of the manor which was later handed over by Edward I to his queen Eleanor who made it over to the monks of Christ Church, Canterbury. After the Dissolution it passed through several hands in a short while, including those of the gallant but luckless Thomas Wyatt, ultimately coming into the possession of the Botelers. Meanwhile the other big house of the neighbourhood, Barham Court, has intriguing legends and histories associated with it, most of them having their origins in Hasted's *History of the County of Kent.*

According to him one of the four Knights involved in the murder of Thomas à Becket was Randal Fitz-Urse; after the fell deed had been accomplished he fled to Ireland, changing his name—while a kinsman, Robert de Barham, from Barham near Canterbury took over the estate. Without going into the full detail of this grisly story and the fate of the four miscreants who hoped by their action to win favour with the King but instead perished on a Crusade, it is sufficient to note that the first time Teston is mentioned in connection with the de Barham family is in 1390. At this time Richard de Barham was Sheriff of Kent and held office at Barham Court. Passing from him to his son Nicholas it presently came into the hands of Henry Barham who married Elizabeth Culpeper, the aunt of the ill-fated Catherine Howard. A later member of the same family was the founder of the Gloucester Furnace mentioned in the previous chapter and also owner of several other furnaces, being reputedly one of the wealthiest people in the Weald. Among other notable members, though of the Canterbury branch of the family, was

West Farleigh cricket ground. *Author's collection*

the Reverend Richard Harris Barham, the author of the *Ingoldsby Legends*. In the early years of James I's reign Anne, heiress of Thomas Barham of Teston married Sir Oliver Boteler, thus linking Barham Court with the manor of Teston.

However those were difficult times; Sir Oliver's second son William, a staunch Royalist, was one of the Kentish gentlemen who presented the Kentish Petition to the House of Commons and was incarcerated in the Fleet prison for his pains. No sooner was he out of that noisome place than a force of Cromwellian soldiery turned up at Barham Court searching for their opponents and looting the house while William who was on his way to join the King at Nottingham had the ill-fortune to be captured en route. After another few months in prison he managed, perhaps by bribing the guard, to get away and enlisted a regiment to serve the King: unhappily he was killed at Cropredy Bridge near Banbury in 1644. A Sir Philip Boteler some fifty years later added Pimp's at East Farleigh and Nettlestead to the estate and did a great deal to improve it; among other things he re-built Teston church, one of the windows of which was transferred to Nettlestead. Another later descendant, a cousin Mrs Elizabeth Bouverie, also did much for the estate, and on her death parts of it were first leased and then sold to an old friend of hers, Admiral Sir Charles Middleton, who was created Lord Barham in 1805.

This astonishing person had a great and lasting influence on the village, for he set about the management of the farms and estate with the same diligence that he had shown when controller of the Navy during the years 1778 to 1790. Prior to that he had been Captain of H.M.S. *Arundel* in 1758 during the Seven Years War, and later was appointed Vice-Admiral in 1793 and Full Admiral in 1795; curiously he never hoisted his flag afloat. He was a junior Lord of the Admiralty in 1805, at the age of seventy-nine! Joan Severn mentions in her book that he achieved a three-fold increase in the yield of the farm and that it was so productive that William Pitt came along to visit it. Among other crops he created a hop-garden of some twenty-five acres and then planted coppices of chestnut to provide the poles, as well as plantations of oak and willow for other purposes. Most of these are still there and are in full production.

Among the ship's company of H.M.S. *Arundel* was a Surgeon James Ramsay who, on return to England with injuries, took Holy Orders and then went out as a clergyman to St Kitts. While there he became interested in the problem of the Africans on the plantations, but having come up against some opposition returned to this country where Sir Charles offered him the living of Teston. At Ramsay's invitation William Wilberforce and other abolitionists frequently met here to discuss their anti-slavery campaign which ultimately led to the abolition of the slave trade in 1833.

Teston was very fortunate in the other later owners of Barham Court. Sir Charles Warde, for instance, followed Lord Barham's example in management of the estate but he did even more for the parish as a whole. The list of his

An old print of East Farleigh Bridge, scene of the famous battle of 1648 when Sir Thomas Fairfax forced his way across. *Kent County Library*

East Farleigh Bridge today, showing strengthening ribs beneath the arches. *Author's collection*

appointments and positions is impressive: A.D.C. to the Governor of Gibraltar, A.D.C. to the G.O.C., Northern Ireland, C.O. of the West Kent Yeomanry, M.P. for Maidstone; these are just a few of them. Similarly there is a great list of improvements made in the village—The Working Men's Club, improvements in the church in conjunction with the Lord of the Manor, Mr Leigh and the Fremlins of Wateringbury, new bungalows built for workers on the estate, the running of Barham Court as a military hospital during the 1914-1918 war. When finally Sir Charles Warde died in 1937 he bequeathed the estate to his wife's cousin, Sir Arthur Stern, who carried on the same tradition of service to the community.

There is one other interesting feature of this village, namely the Cricket Ball factory, a surprising thing to find in such rural surroundings. Yet Alfred Reader & Co. Ltd have been making cricket and hockey balls since 1808 and their products go all over the world. Founded as William Martin & Son the business had first been established at Hadlow in 1808 but had later moved to Teston where Thomas Martin ran the village shop and Post Office as well as making cricket balls. In due course Alfred Reader, whose family had come down hop-picking each year, bought the shop; and, on the death of Thomas Martin, also took on the manufacture of cricket balls. Now still a family firm it makes some 65,000 a year; and this and Duke's at Chiddingstone Causeway are the principal surviving hand-sewn cricket ball manufacturers.

The lovely sweep of river round to Barming, where there was once another Roman villa, and to East Farleigh leads to yet one more of the fine medieval bridges, some say the most beautiful of all. Certainly the setting of the East Farleigh bridge is most attractive, with timber framed buildings, many trees and barns and farms to the south. There was a Priory here and also the manor house of Gallants which again was the property of the ubiquitous Culpeper family. The bridge, as usual, has massive cut-waters but in this case there is no special refuge for pedestrians although the road-surface is only eleven feet wide. There is another interesting feature of this bridge also, and that is the way in which stone ribs stretch the length of the pointed arches. But the angle of approach by road at either end is awkward and much skilful engineering work has had to be undertaken, including a small extra arch. Unhappily the view to the north is less attractive, spoiled by the railway, and all these bridges carry much motor traffic.

We are still deep in the heart of the hop country but Maidstone is now close at hand, and the contrasting world of industry lies only a mile away from this idyllic tranquillity. Yet Farleigh Bridge is famous for something quite the reverse of peaceful, the advance of the army of Sir Thomas Fairfax and the attack on Maidstone of 1648.

No story of our river would be complete without some reference to this stirring action although the details of it are well known and have been recorded by many authors, Clarendon among them. However it is interesting that two particular assembly points were used on this occasion, places which have seen great gatherings of Kentish people in many critical moments. These are Barham Downs and Penenden Heath.

In May of that year, 1648, there was a great rising of Royalists in Kent, many places like Sittingbourne and Faversham were seized, and a meeting was held at Tunstall near Sittingbourne where young Squire Hales was chosen as leader. A further rally took place later in the month at Canterbury and a force collected on Barham Downs, famous as the scene of British resistance to the first invasion by Julius Caesar. Unhappily already there was some dispute as to the leadership and when word came that none other than Sir Thomas Fairfax was advancing to put down the rising, it was decided that Squire Hales was too inexperienced and Lord Holland was chosen as Commander-in-Chief. He in turn selected the Earl of Norwich as his General and by the 1st of June the army of the Royalists was encamped on the traditional meeting place outside Maidstone, Penenden Heath. From there Norwich sent out detachments to hold Aylesford and Maidstone bridges but he had too few men under arms to make any place reasonably secure—and worse still, he soon received news that Fairfax was making for Farleigh Bridge. A force was hurriedly sent to hold it and a desperate fight ensued before Fairfax and the Parliamentary army manged to force their way across. Even then all was not easy for them as all along the road to Tovil and at the crossing of the Loose river there were hurriedly raised barricades; but the dash and courage of the Royalists was insufficient to cope with the superior training and discipline of the Roundheads who slowly but surely forced their way on, at length storming Maidstone in the late evening. This was the final blow to the Royal cause in Kent . . . So these old stones of Farleigh Bridge have seen desperate action and great valour in days gone by.

CHAPTER SIX

The County Town and its Neighbourhood

FOR MANY people who hurry daily to their work in the shops and offices of busy Maidstone, the river is mainly something they have to cross on their way. The same was certainly true for countless families making the journey down from London to the coast in the years before and after the last war when massive traffic jams used to build up on the A20 with vehicles creeping forward nose-to-tail over the Maidstone bridge. The M20 and the new bridge have made a vast difference to the speedy passage across the river but the rapid circulation scarcely gives an opportunity to reflect what the town must have been like some one hundred and fifty years ago, with a population of only about eight thousand. Nor is there time to reflect that within a mile or so up-river there is the remarkable Loose valley with its picturesque little village and the curious stream which manages to fall some 150 feet in only three miles. After rising at Langley and proceeding in a normal manner as far as Brishing Court it suddenly starts to behave like a stream in the Pennines or on the Mendip hills and vanishes into a swallet or swallow-hole only to reappear and supply numerous ponds in the neighbourhood of the village of Loose before heading off down the valley on its way to join the Medway.

The secret of this behaviour is, of course, that Kentish rag-stone, the natural rock of these hills, is a type of lime-stone and the Loose stream follows lines of faulting accordingly, just as does the subterranean river Axe in Wookey Hole in Somerset. There, as is the case here, is a famous paper-mill using water from the Axe for various processes. However with the Loose stream, though there are plenty of hidden culverts and cellars where old pumps used to supply water to the mills and houses, there are as far as is known no great series of underground caverns nor legends of witches. Nevertheless it is a most attractive valley rich in the unusual, quiet within a mile of bustle and noise, saved from the main rush of traffic by the viaduct erected by Thomas Telford in 1829 which carries the main A229 clear of the village.

It has been suggested, not altogether seriously, that the name might be derived from the way in which the stream loses itself. But it is more likely that it comes from a synonym for a sty, as Roger Higham puts forward in his book *Kent*, as this was in earlier times a farming community with several tanneries with the hides hanging out to dry on tenterhooks, a village forge and no less than thirty kilns for drying hops of which there were 150 acres in the parish.

The fifteenth century wool house is a half-timbered building originally connected with the cleansing of wool, and from Lambarde's reference in 1576 in *Perambulations of Kent* in which he stated that the Loose stream drove thirteen fulling mills and one corn mill it will be appreciated what a very busy area this was in earlier years. In addition to all this, the main road between Maidstone and Linton, leading on eventually to the wool centre of Cranbrook, used to pass through the village and half-a-dozen trace horses were kept at the ready to help waggons up the very steep Old Loose Hill. As if the abrupt slope of the hill was not enough, water from the stream would flood across the lowest stretch and make it necessary to have blocks ready to put behind wheels if the horses began to slip. Probably some very weary waggoners would drop in at the *Chequers Inn* after a long haul through from the Weald to fortify themselves ready for the struggle up the hill.

The interesting operation known as fulling comes into the story of our river to such an increasing extent now that this would seem to be a good moment to take a closer look at it. After the woollen cloth had been woven, quite a cottage industry this, it had to be cleansed from all the dirt and grease and there were no bleaches or detergents in the thirteenth and fourteenth centuries. When the Flemish weavers came over they had recourse to an

Near Loose village, where the waters of the Loose stream emerge. *Author's collection*

absorbent clay containing hydrated silica and alumina, still known today as fuller's earth, and which has highly absorbent properties. The principal sources of this material were in the parish of Boxley and in the neighbourhood of Leeds, Kent. J. M. Preston in his *Industrial Medway* refers to a Mr John Watts who in 1704 bought the estate in Boxley where the earth was to be found at a depth of 30 feet and duly mined it; however, there was certainly much digging for it long before Mr Watts came on the scene.

The cloth would be put into troughs with water and this clay solution and there pounded with beaters driven by the water-wheel or sometimes kneaded by being trampled by human feet. After this cleansing process had been completed the cloth was strung out on tenterhooks to dry and stretch before the final processes of teasing with teazles,* to raise the nap, shearing and colouring. An interesting battery of trade-names originate from this: Fuller, Walker and Shearer. It will be easy to see how, when the cloth industry began to decline with the transfer of the works to the north of the country, these fulling mills could be adapted to the pulping of rag and other material for the manufacture of paper.

This is what happened in the Loose valley. Lambarde's numbering seems to have been faulty as the highest possible site for a mill up the Loose stream

*Dipsocus fullonum, fuller's teasel, the heads of which have hooked prickles.

Pear blossom and oasthouse at Barming. *Author's collection*

Great Ivy Mill today. *Author's collection*

would be at what has been called Leg-o-Mutton pond and there are only thirteen mill sites all told from there to the junction with the Medway, one less than Lambarde suggests. However the operations of these thirteen have been most thoroughly surveyed, with the conclusion that No 4, the Loose village mill, was a corn mill right through its history. In most informative articles R. J. Spain in *Arch. Cant* in 1972 and 1973 examined their ownership and development over the years, several interesting facts emerging among others that James Whatman, so well known for his high quality hand-made paper, worked No 2, the Upper Mill, between 1774 and 1793 when he retired and the business moved to Turkey Mill on the Ashford road. Much more will be said about him later. Upper Mill was a short way upstream from the viaduct and seems to have been altered to a corn mill in 1851 under William Wilson, finally closing down in 1908. Further down stream was Little Ivy Mill passing through a variety of hands including Smith and Allnutt from 1653 onward, and ranging from fulling to corn-milling, paper-making and then back to corn. There is in existence an advertisement for the sale of this property in which reference is made to "the good head of water from the never-failing Loose stream— ". Finally, in about 1912 it was converted into a dwelling house, one of the two mill ponds being filled in but the other still a fine pond, kept clean by "resident swans" and apparently abounding in all manner of fish. This mill and its neighbour Great Ivy Mill, which was also at one time in the hands of Smith and Allnutt, owe their names to the fact that a certain Thomas Pine once owned them; his house in Cripple Street, Loose, was covered in ivy and was known as Ivy House. Great Ivy, occupied by a fuller, William Lane, in 1638, changed to paper-making in 1685 under Richard Burnham, and is thus one of the nine oldest paper mills in the county. After Thomas Pine, Smith and Allnutt moved in in 1815. By 1873 Barcham Green had it and the mill continued making paper until 1911, a total period of some two hundred and twenty-five years. It was then demolished but to-day the foreman's house is a good example of a fine weather-boarded dwelling house. In R. J. Spain's article it is noted that Cherry Kearton, whose books on animal behaviour were so popular in the 1930s, once lived here with his chimpanzee Mary.

Of the other mills, Hayle Mill was first fulling and then altered to paper-making under the Green family and is still operated by Barcham Green; Upper and Lower Crisbrook were first fulling mills and then converted to corn, one of the Tovil mills when paper-making under Thomas Pine was damaged in the explosion of a gunpowder mill in 1731. This last must have been the Bridge mill which switched from fulling to the making of gunpowder and was then adapted for the production of vegetable oils—linseed and oilseed rape. Finally Albert E. Reed took it over in 1899 and converted it to paper manufacture. In an interesting test quoted by R. J. Spain Reeds discovered that the volume of water passing through Crisbrook pond gave a flow of 1,300 gallons a minute so the "never failing Loose stream" provided a wonderful source of water-power and a valuable supply for the washing and other necessary features of a paper-mill. Above everything else these Tovil mills had the great advantage of close proximity to the main stream of the Medway and hence their products could be loaded easily into barges for transit to the river mouth and so to the great market of London.

It was the rapid growth of the metropolis over the centuries as a commercial centre that had such a great influence on the trade of Maidstone, for the county town has always been closely associated with manufacture and commercial undertakings of every kind.

Teignmouth Shore in *Kent* says of Maidstone, "There is something fairly picturesque but not really beautiful about its narrow streets, and open market place; an old county-town atmosphere pervades it." This may have been true at the beginning of the century but now the whole impression is one of bustle. Big new office blocks have gone up, a multi-storey car-park broods over the southern side of King Street, there are large stores, the West Kent Hospital, the County Hall and the Town Hall and now, to relieve traffic congestion, an additional bridge so that the Medway is crossed by two road-bridges side by side. Around and about, among hurrying shoppers and office workers, cars and buses circulate rapidly. It is a far cry from the days when "hogges" roamed about the streets during the night as well as by day as Dorothy Gardiner so amusingly records in her *Companion into Kent*. Yet even at the time of the Domesday survey there were five corn mills listed as being in Maidstone, so as far back as 1085 the place must have had a considerable population and probably a corn trade down the Medway. It would be utterly impossible to cover all the many aspects of the town adequately in such a restricted space as this or to show in full how great has been the influence of the river on its development. One of the most important tributaries of the Medway, the River Len, flows in close to the town bridge and its course, notable buildings and characters connected with it will be described in a later chapter. It must be sufficient to say here that the corn and fulling mills of the Len would have added considerably to the importance of Maidstone as a trading centre. There was, too, its very crucial position so far as roads were concerned, for the Roman road from Watling Street to the south coast came down Bluebell Hill, passing through Week Street and Stone Street. In addition, just to the north, but now of course absorbed into the town, was the traditional meeting place of the Jutish tribesmen, Penenden Heath—of which now only a small area remains unbuilt on. Against the date 1073 the *Anglo Saxon Chronicle* records that there was "a great council at a place called

Maidstone Bridge from upstream, showing the riverside walks. *Author's collection*

Maidstone — Archbishop's Palace, All Saints' Church and College. *Author's collection*

Penenden Heath" at which the Archbishop of Canterbury Lanfranc asserted the rights of the Church in the tenure of land.

The Archbishops of Canterbury had a particular influence on the early history of Maidstone as they were Lords and Patrons of the whole town. Archbishop Boniface founded a hospital in 1245, Archbishop Courtenay obtained permission from Richard II to carry out alterations to the Parish Church to make it more in keeping with the importance of the place. This was the origin of the very fine church of All Saints, rebuilt in the early fifteenth century in the Perpendicular style, on the site of the earlier church beside the river. Archbishop Courtenay also obtained authority to establish a College of secular canons under a Master, the first of whom, John Wootton, was buried in All Saints. Another learned divine who was also Master a little later, William Grocyn, was buried here. A friend of Erasmus, and teacher of Sir Thomas More, he was one of the band of great scholars whose work led to the Renaissance after the fall of Constantinople in 1451. The ragstone walls of the collegiate buildings and the fine gate-tower still throw their reflections into the limpid waters of the river, while the centre for Kent Rural Music is housed inside.

An old print of the medieval Maidstone bridge. *Kent County Library*

Northward of All Saints Church is the Archbishop's Palace, also lying right beside the river, which was started by Archbishop Ufford and completed by his successor Simon Islip in about 1350. In the reign of Henry VII Archbishop Morton, whose financial capabilities proved so invaluable to the Tudor monarchs, set about a detailed overhaul and improvement of it; it was his splendid building together with the range of stables, the huge tithe barn and the spacious gardens which passed into the hands of the King at the time of the Dissolution of the Monasteries and were then granted by Edward VI to Sir Thomas Wyatt. These buildings and gardens beside the river in all their beauty, together with the Parish Church and the College, have been spoken of as the finest group of medieval buildings in the south of England, and here it is, too, that the Len slides in to join the main stream. One other ancient construction used to stand nearby, possibly even built by Archbishop Ufford or Archbishop Islip as Samuel Ireland, in his *Picturesque View of the River Medway*, suggested. This was the Great Bridge which stood with six small almshouses perched upon it. Then, when it was becoming rather decayed, repair work and re-building were undertaken in 1808 in which state it lasted until 1879 when a new bridge was built alongside it to the design of Sir Joseph Bazalgette. So for a short while about a hundred years ago there were two bridges side by side before the earlier one was demolished, just as we have two today.

The ancient palace of the Archbishops passed through several hands, including those of Thomas Astley who in turn passed it over to his brother Sir John who was Master of the Queen's Jewels and who had already been granted Allington Castle by Queen Elizabeth I. Mistress Astley's gardens became a place of resort for the people of Maidstone during this time, when the population of the town was only some two to three thousand, and the four town wharfs did a lively trade in corn, cloth, fuller's earth, Kentish ragstone and timber—not forgetting the hops, of course. There were five locally registered hoys which could get up as far as Maidstone, lowering their gear to come under the bridges at Rochester, Aylesford and, if need be, Maidstone as well. The old palace of the Archbishops remained with various branches of the same family of Astley during the succeeding reigns, the most famous being Jacob Astley who was created a Baron in 1644. As a young man he had gained military experience in the Low Countries and also with the renowned Gustavus Adolphus of Sweden; in which service his career was an interesting parallel with that of Prince Rupert who also learned his cavalry tactics in that hard school. Back they both came to fight for the King, Astley holding a series of commands and being in the thick of a host of actions. His prayer before the battle of Edgehill is well-known, "Lord I shall be very busy this day . . . I may forget Thee; do not Thou forget me." In Lord Macaulay's stirring poem, "The Battle of Naseby" it is only natural that he should feature in the first verse—

"It was about the noon of a glorious day of June
That we saw their banners dance and their cuirasses shine,
And the Man of Blood was there, with his long essenced hair,
And Astley, and Sir Marmaduke and Rupert of the Rhine."

Obviously Oliver Cromwell, that stern and rigorous leader of the Parliamentary forces and later of the country, must have appreciated his great qualities for he allowed him to return to the old palace on parole after the final collapse of the Royal cause; there he lived quietly till his death in 1651.

The old palace, the precincts, gardens and the old mill are now corporation property, the last mentioned being the cause of the nearby road being named Mill Street. Close too, also, is the Len bridge, possibly even older than the original Maidstone bridge. Other corporation property of note includes the fine Elizabethan building Chillington House which contains the Museum and Art Gallery, and of course the magnificent Mote Park, formerly the estate of Lord Rivers, who was guardian of the little Princes later murdered in the Tower, which embodies among other things a lake and a county cricket ground. No Kentish town could be without that!

I mentioned earlier how important Penenden Heath was as a meeting place, and in this we must not lose sight of the part it played as an assembly point for the peasants' rebellion when Wat Tyler led his tragic host on the road to London in 1381 after the release of the orator and preacher John Ball from the dungeons below the Archbishop's Palace. Only about a hundred years after this daring endeavour which had such dire consequences for Tyler when he was cut down by Walworth, the Lord Mayor of London—and for so many of the unfortunate participants—another assembly took place. The reason for this can be traced back to the later years of the Wars of the Roses, to the marriage of the Lady Elizabeth Grey, née Woodville, to the Yorkist King Edward IV and to the position of honour and trust conferred upon her father, Lord Rivers of the Mote, as well as other members of the Woodville family. It is well known how this enraged the Earl of Warwick, known as the King Maker, who began to plot to restore the Lancastrian Henry VI to the throne, in the course of which a posse of his friends invaded Mote Park and ransacked the house. It was not long before the unfortunate Henry had been put back on the throne and Warwick had had Lord Rivers beheaded.

However Warwick was not left long in charge of affairs for with the return of Edward IV, his victory at Barnet and the death of Warwick in the battle, the Woodvilles were restored to their position of eminence, and Sir Anthony Woodville had succeeded his beheaded father as Lord Rivers, and proud owner of the Mote. He was known as a fine scholar and was one of the patrons of the printer William Caxton, but his position in history is much more assured by his actions on the death of the Yorkist monarch Edward IV.

As guardian of the little Yorkist Prince Edward, his nephew, the heir to the throne, he set out at once for London with him from Ludlow but was met on the way by the boy's uncle Richard of Gloucester, who assumed custody of the Prince and arrested Rivers. The stage was thus set for the mysterious death of the two boy Princes in the Tower of London, and within a fortnight Rivers and all his chief supporters had been executed.

Nevertheless one very important relative of the Woodvilles was in Richard of Gloucester's confidence. This was the Duke of Buckingham who was married to Katharine, sister of the widowed Queen and who was also, possibly due to unsatisfied ambition, becoming disillusioned with his brother-in-law Richard. Another actor in the plot was the wary and versatile Bishop Morton, previously mentioned, who was later such a notable adviser to Henry Tudor and who influenced Buckingham to switch his allegiance to the Lancastrian cause.

The Mote once again became the centre for an uprising in the south-east, the plan being that Buckingham was to raise the West Country, Henry, Earl of Richmond, the Lancastrian claimant to the throne was to land in the West with his fleet from Brittany, while Sir Richard Woodville of the Mote raised the men of Kent.

Alas for the plans so carefully hatched. Floods from the terrible October storms prevented Buckingham from crossing the Severn and he was caught in

Shropshire. Henry never landed, his fleet being scattered by the bad weather; and the men of Kent gathering on Penenden Heath marched to Gravesend on the way to London but then dispersed on hearing of Buckingham's capture. Thus the plot came to a sad end and it was not until nearly two years afterwards that Henry of Richmond triumphed at Bosworth Field (22nd August 1485), establishing himself as the first of the great Tudor dynasty with the aid of Sir Richard Woodville of the Mote and other members of the family who had fled to the Continent to join his forces.

In this way Maidstone was at the very centre of affairs at a crucial time in English history; Penenden Heath, too, saw the massing of Kentish forces in support of Sir Thomas Wyatt's luckless endeavour to prevent Mary Tudor's marriage to the Spanish King Philip. He will come into the picture again in the next chapter; but Penenden now is only a shadow of its former self though there are still noble trees and grassy sward. The contrast between these historic places, the Heath, the Mote, the old Palace and the humming modern town is staggering, as remarkable as the increase in population from three thousand in Elizabeth I's reign to something in the region of seventy thousand now. Remarkable also is the variety of industry that has been centred on Maidstone in the course of the years, industries which provide perhaps the greatest contrast of all with the concept of an old county town. From the ragstone quarries of medieval times providing not only building materials but also cannon balls, every possible variation in manufacture and trade seems to have occurred, increasing in importance at one period, later in decline, only to be succeeded by something equally profitable. Agricultural machinery, paper, cement, confectionery—the list is endless. The final contrast is to go along a very short distance down the river as far as the *Malta Inn* at Allington to see the Medway given over entirely to motor boats, other small craft and all the delight of high summer by the river-side, the towpaths alive with cheerful crowds rejoicing in the glint of flashing water amid the cool green of the trees.

Maidstone bridge as rebuilt in 1808. *Kent County Library*

CHAPTER SEVEN

The Limit of the Tidal Flow

THE NAVIGATION of the early hoys of Elizabethan times must have presented many difficulties. The banks of the Medway were reported as being irregular and much broken and, with no tow-path, the vessels would have been largely dependent upon the tide. Thus they would drift up or down, more or less controlled by their crews labouring at the sweeps, perhaps running up a corner of sail to give steerage way in between the bridges, then dropping all gear abruptly as they shot the arches.

For a busy port like Maidstone to be so entirely dependent upon the tide was clearly a great handicap, so during the reign of Charles I steps were taken to introduce locks and a tow-path and by Charles II's time a second Act in this connection had been passed through Parliament. In due course, instead of the very strong tidal flow coming up as far as East Farleigh, another lock was constructed near the Archbishop's Palace at Maidstone, but when Allington Lock was made in 1792 this was no longer necessary. Nevertheless, despite all difficulties the variety of trade on the river was considerable, Hasted giving us corn, grain, hay, hops, wool, leather, all manner of provisions, coal, lime from chalk dug at Rochester and sent to Essex, Suffolk and Norfolk . . . and quarry stone. To this can be added fuller's earth, timber, fruit, silica sand and all manner of iron goods. John Harris in his *History of Kent* quoted by J. M. Preston in *Industrial Medway* refers to one of the obstacles, the Aylesford bridge, as "a very fair and large stone bridge . . . the arches whereof are so high that a large hoy can pass through with her mast lowered down".

In the earlier years before any records of navigation on the river, one of the first fords downstream from Maidstone was at Allington where a side-track from the Pilgrims' Way would seem to have crossed. Traces of a late Bronze Age settlement came to light when the railway engineers were laying their track in the eighteen fifties, and some one hundred yards south-west of the walls of Allington Castle were found the remains of a Roman villa. It has been suggested that this might possibly have been the dwelling of an overseer of the quarries, as Kentish ragstone has been worked for many centuries in this neighbourhood. The Roman wall of London was largely built of this material and as this was the nearest source of supply it could well have been quarried here and then taken down the Medway and round to London.

Close to Allington Lock, concealed behind the line of tall poplars that fringe the river bank the crenellated towers and walls of the old castle loom amid the clustered greenery, a peaceful haven in startling contrast to the tearing vehicles that roar across the concrete span of the M20 bridge not far away. Here the Carmelite Order, the white friars, maintain a conference centre, a meeting place for all types of people in the Christian world who can there find refreshment and inspiration within these massive walls. They know, too, that they are privileged to be sharing living history for the old Kentish ragstone blocks have witnessed many daring plans in the making and been associated with many eminent men.

There is sure to have been a strong point of some kind here during the Jutish times for it would be necessary to command the ford, and certainly the Norman nobles who owned the place in succession, the formidable Odo of Bayeux and the powerful William, Earl de Warrenne, among them, raised a motte, a moated mound, as their stronghold. The Domesday survey entry regarding Allington is rather amusing in that it details the following: "15 villains with two bordars, they have one team and a half. A church there. And two slaves. And half a mill. And one dene (clearing) of 15 shillings. Wood of 8 hogs. And an acre of meadow . . . Uluric held it of Alnud Cilt." One can only guess that the "half mill" must have been the half on one bank of the river and half on the other, hence owned by two different people, perhaps in different estates. As to who Alnud Cilt can be there have been many conjectures—some suggest Ulnoth, the fourth son of Earl Godwin. Anyhow, at the time of the

River Medway—looking across from Allington Marina. *Author's collection*

Conquest the Estate was seized and passed over to Odo, from him to de Warrenne and then on via a daughter to one Sir Giles de Allington whose son William was unwise or lawless enough to build a private fortress without the King's permission. Undoubtedly this was done during that desperate period in Stephen's reign when every individual nobleman acted as a local robber-baron throwing up a castle from which he could dart out in strength to loot and pillage. These "adulterine castles" as they were termed were one of the first items on the list for attention on the Plantagenet Henry II's accession; so in 1174 it was duly torn down.

This same William de Allington is also sometimes referred to as "de Columbariis", a name which may be associated with the two ancient dove-cots or columbaria which Lord Conway suggests are among the oldest in England, being built in the twelfth century. Doves and pigeons seem to be inextricably linked with the story of Allington for Sir Henry Wyatt, a later owner, is supposed to have been fed with pigeons caught by his cat when a prisoner in the Tower of London; and Sir Thomas Wyatt brought some brown pigeons from Italy in 1526. These, as Carmelite Father McGreal writes in the guide book to the castle, have been bred at Allington ever since.

Some traces remain of the manor-house which succeeded the adulterine castle, notably in the gate-house. Then in the reign of Edward I Stephen de Penchester, Lord of Penshurst, whom we have already met, applied for and obtained a licence to crenellate. At once the gate tower was strengthened, curtain walls and towers, altogether eight in number, were added and in the southwest corner what is known as Soloman's Tower was adapted as a Keep. The defensive works were completed by a channel cut through from the river to provide an encircling moat. Lord Conway, who did so much to restore the castle in the early twentieth century, noted the interesting fact that the earlier Penchester fortifications were roughly built of Kentish ragstone while later work made use of very hard brick, neatly set in remarkably durable mortar. This brick-work he associates with similar work of similar date in southern Normandy. A solid drain of massive stones led beneath the shafts from the upper floor garderobe in the guard tower into the moat.

After de Penchester's death his widow Margaret continued to hold the castle for the rest of her life after which it passed via a daughter, Joan, to Sir Henry de Cobham, Chief Justiciar of England, who held among other appointments the position of Constable of Dover, Rochester and Tonbridge castles. For the following one hundred and fifty years his descendants held the place but apparently no new work or even repairs were carried out during this time, and a considerable amount of damage was sustained, very likely during the Wars of the Roses.

Lambarde writing in 1570 refers to certain gentlemen of Kent as being "not so ancient stocks as elsewhere, especially in the parts nearer to London from which city courtiers, lawyers and merchants be continually translated, and do become new plants among them." This comment could certainly apply to Lord Barham at Teston who was mentioned in the last chapter, but what a transformation that particular "new plant" made to the village. The same is true of the new owner of Allington, for Sir Henry Wyatt who purchased the castle in 1492 was the rather unlikely combination of a Yorkshireman who was the loyal supporter of the Lancastrian—or Tudor—Henry VII. On the other hand, it was the Yorkist King who had consigned him to the Tower so his dislike of the Yorkist cause is understandable.

Sir Henry set about the general overhaul and improvement of the castle, knocking out the old narrow windows and substituting the larger Tudor style, erecting state apartments on the north east side, adding a gallery to the Great Hall, and putting up an entirely new building known as the Tudor House whose lath and plaster work forms a pleasant contrast to the grey stone of the main courtyard. The Long Gallery, now used as a conference room, was also added by him. Remaining in royal favour until his death in 1537, he was visited here by the shrewd and calculating Henry VII, and these old walls also echoed to the rumbling tones of the ebullient Henry VIII and his mighty minister Thomas Wolsey. It is interesting how many of our Medway castles and houses have welcomed the Tudor monarchs and their ministers; and here, at Allington, that young and flighty lady Anne Boleyn might well have come a-visiting also, as Sir Henry's son Thomas was her lover before Henry VIII. Sir Thomas, in spite of this, seems to have been used on embassies by the king and when the monasteries were dissolved, he received Boxley, Malling and Aylesford though his greater fame is as a poet. In 1544 yet another royal visitor, Queen Catherine Parr, was entertained here and it is recorded that 7s.4d. (36.6p) was charged for making ready her dinner. His courtier son, Sir Thomas the younger, was a distinguished soldier who was appointed Sheriff of Kent in Edward VI's reign. His desperate attempt to influence the course of policy by raising the standard of revolt on Penenden Heath and marching at the head of the Kentish rebels to prevent the Spanish marriage of Queen Mary to Philip of Spain ended in disaster. He met his end gallantly, declaring that the "Lady Elizabeth had no knowledge of the uprising", but his action meant the block for the luckless Jane Grey and her husband Lord Guildford Dudley, and a spell of incarceration and cross-examination for Elizabeth from which she only escaped through her unerring political instinct and cleverness. Tom Wyatt's ill-conceived action so nearly deprived this country of the great age of Elizabeth I. Passing to the crown, the castle was later granted to Sir John Astley who lived in the Old Palace, Maidstone, leaving Allington leased to various occupiers. Later still the Romneys owned it, the buildings decayed, parts were used as farms and moves were set on foot to demolish and use the stones as building material. Luckily local outcry and a lawyer, Mr Dudley

Aylesford village, church and medieval bridge, from an old print. *Kent County Library*

Falke, checked this outrage, repairs were undertaken and at length Lord Conway was able to purchase it in 1905 and restore it, also buying up and removing the assorted factory-yards and houses that had been erected between the castle and the river. It is due very largely to his drive and foresight that the castle stands today enshrined in its trees with grassy lawns alongside the lock and stately poplars lining the Medway bank without the ugly mercantile bustle that could so easily have spoiled this stretch of the busy river.

Only two miles further downstream is Sir Thomas Wyatt's other possession, Aylesford, where there is a Carmelite Friary and yet another medieval bridge with the fine old church tower overlooking it. Exactly who was the builder of this is not certain; perhaps it was the work of the "Hospitarii Pontifices" connected with the monks of Rochester. However there it stands a narrow roadway with the usual refuges for foot passengers, massive masonry and originally six arches now reduced to five as the two in the centre were altered into one to facilitate the passage of barges. But even so there is only ten feet of headroom so any hoy or barge would need to have all her gear neatly lowered in order to work through in safety. Here also, contrary to the state of affairs in the upper reaches of the river, the question of tides assumes importance, with an ebb tide running for nine hours at Allington and a flood for only three. To a certain extent, of course, the tidal flow has been altered by the embanking and improvement alongside the Medway, the result of modern industrialisation, with wharves and factory sites, some no longer in use but many fully operational. All this is very different from the times when Elizabethan hoys worked their way up between the "irregular and broken banks" and the containment of the river has tended to push the tide further and further inland.

This little town of Aylesford, so close to Maidstone and greatly afflicted by the nearby industrial development down-river, is the site of a very ancient and important crossing, a good shallow ford and the last for some nine miles—in fact until Rochester is reached. The stones of Kit's Coty House stand right alongside the old track leading up from the ford, the White Horse Stone in folk-lore connected with the great battle between Vortigern King of Kent and the Jutish host. Possibly, as was suggested in Chapter one, the Pilgrims' Way may have crossed the Medway here, though the rocky river-bed at Snodland is on an even more direct course.

Aylesford bridge—upstream side, iron ties and cutwaters, the tide about three quarters flood and the banks very muddy. *Author's collection*

Possibly there was a wooden bridge prior to the medieval one but that is uncertain. What is historically definite is that Baron de Grey allowed a group of Carmelite hermits to journey to Aylesford in 1242, having granted them land on the river bank for their settlement. Here they constructed a small chapel surrounded by a number of individual cells and, in August 1248, the Bishop of Rochester consecrated it, dedicating it to the Assumption of the Glorious Virgin. Throughout succeeding generations the de Grey family offered additional help to the Friary, gifts of grain and hay from their other estates in Kent and Essex, gifts of money for the repair of buildings, annual benefactions of all sorts. By 1417 a new church had been constructed and the Friary had been granted lands in Burham from which fresh water could be piped. However all the time the community was very poor, as the visiting commissioners found when they were assessing the value of the monasteries in the country at the time of the Dissolution. In 1538 the community was disbanded and the property passed into the hands of Sir Thomas Wyatt and, after his son's death on the scaffold, to the Crown. Some years later Queen Elizabeth I granted it to Sir John Sedley who turned it into his family residence. All this time there had been additions made at intervals, and now Sir John carried out many alterations to make it more convenient as a dwelling, also adding a farm near the entrance to the Friary. After the Sedleys it passed to Sir Peter Ricaut, a Dutch financier, and during the Civil War was the scene of excitement far removed from the life of prayer and contemplation of the original Friary. Sir Peter was known as a keen Royalist so to forestall a Kentish uprising a body of Parliamentary troops was sent to search the place soon after the beginning of the war. Finding a hidden cache of arms, Sir Peter and his wife were taken to be interned in Upnor Castle but on the way their coachman made a gallant effort to escape. A furious chase developed through the streets of Maidstone but at length they were caught. Thereafter the building was used by the Parliamentary forces, sometimes as a meeting place for the Commissioners for Kent, at times as an arsenal of arms and ammunition for the Parliamentary Army. Twice local Royalists tried to capture it, and on a third occasion, in 1648, it was seized when the Earl of Norwich sent a force of 1,000 men to hold Aylesford Bridge. However, as we have seen already, Sir Thomas Fairfax managed to cross Farleigh Bridge and by his capture of Maidstone put an end to the uprising.

Fortunately for the Friary it was, after the Restoration, purchased by a local merchant, Sir John Banks, who set about making it into a fine family mansion, adding a new wing, fitting the old dwellings with panelling and moulded ceilings, landscaping the gardens. Samuel Pepys on a visit to these parts described it as "mightily finely placed by the river." He added "he (Sir John) keeps the grounds about it and walls and the house very handsome . . . ". Thereafter passing through many hands and rented to various tenants in the nineteenth century it was severely damaged by fire in 1930. Nothing daunted, the then owner Mr Copley Hewitt and his wife set about the work of restoration, finding suitable old beams to replace those burnt in the fire by purchasing the old wooden ship *Arethusa*, having her towed up-river and dismantling her timbers at the riverside outside the Friars. Used by the Army during the last war it again became dilapidated but when put up for sale in 1949 Carmelites all over the world subscribed to buy back their traditional home. So in October of that year Prior Father Malachy Lynch and a small group began the work which has led to the rebirth of the Friars as the place of prayer that it is to-day.

Before we leave the area round about Maidstone to swirl down river among the great paper-mills, cement works and other industrial undertakings, we must inspect the course of the other main tributary of the Medway, the little river Len. It flows through what Teignmouth Shore in his book *Kent* calls "a country of churches and castles, of parks and village greens; a beautiful, homely, healthy, and comfortable country; nothing in it of the wild or gloomy, but very much of the gracious and lovely—a country to be visited at any season of the year with profit and delight." What he did not add was that this country is also rich in history, its buildings speaking of the great figures of by-gone days and above all of King Henry VIII. He must have known this valley of the river Len well for Leeds was his favourite castle, on which he lavished much care and

Modern Allington. These peaceful tree-fringed moorings are just upstream from the castle. *Author's collection*

many additions to the separate tower known as the Gloriette and other parts. Along this valley also lies Hollingbourne, the main seat of the Culpeper family whom we have already encountered in many other areas, whose principal houses were Greenway Court and the Manor and where the fifteenth century church has many memorials to them. Here Henry VIII's fifth wife Catherine Howard spent much of her childhood for her mother Joyce was of another branch of the same family. Also here lay the great Priory of Leeds of which one of the most noted Priors was Anthony St Leger who later obtained the grant of the estate at the Dissolution when it came into the hands of the Crown and was sold to a private individual. This priory, founded like the castle by Robert de Crèvecoeur, was one of the richest houses of the Augustinian canons in Kent. However not all the notable figures that roam these dells and lush fields are monarchs or mighty men of valour. In Broomfield there lived a family of bell-founders, the Hatch family, in the seventeenth century, and all down the valley right through to the Mote and the Len's junction with the Medway there were mills, some owned by the Church or Crown in medieval times, many passing through the hands of successive millers well known in the local community. But not only corn mills were here. Just as with the other tributary rivers of the Medway, there were fulling mills for the cleansing of woollen goods; in fact the Len was known all through the Weald as a special centre for fulling for there were rich deposits of fuller's earth in the neighbourhood of Leeds, and the flow of water was unfailing even in dry weather. Furley in his *History of the Weald of Kent* recorded that the fulling mills were similar to the corn mills except for the mechanism driving the mill-stones and corn hoppers and that in the fourteenth century corn was sometimes ground and clothes fulled by the revolution of the same wheel.

Rising in the neighbourhood of Harrietsham, with brooks and streamlets joining from either side, the Len flows in a more or less westerly direction, dammed into mill ponds here and there, working its way through the countryside on a course approximately parallel with the A20. Many of the twenty-seven mills recorded down the valley are of very ancient date, a large number referred to in the Domesday survey. For example there were stated to be four mills in Harrietsham. However it is usually possible only to trace their history back to the seventeenth or eighteenth centuries; where the buildings still exist they are usually of brick, with weatherboard on the upper storeys. The mill-stones, Derbyshire Peak stones or French burr, are still there in some cases, and the apple wood cogs on the gear wheels, but some mills have been converted into dwellings. From exhaustive surveys made by R. H. Goodsall and R. J. Spain it is apparent that this attractive valley must have been bustling with activity throughout the sixteenth and seventeenth centuries. Nearly every village must have had its corn mill, sometimes worked by the local baker, and several of them the property of the owners of Leeds Castle.

Aylesford medieval bridge, downstream side, showing the widened central arch.
Author's collection

Such a one was Chegworth Mill, first referred to in about 1200, but purchased in 1657 by Sir Cheney Culpeper then at Leeds, yet another member of the famous family. In 1967 this was still in working order and was then owned by Lady Baillie of Leeds. There were a number of mills directly connected with the castle, the "Mille", Keeper's Cottage, and Hollingbourne Manor which was a corn mill all its life, becoming derelict by 1933. Leeds Priory had two corn mills of its own, the Abbey Mill coming into the hands of the Crown at the Dissolution. Later sold to Sir William Meredith it then came into the ownership of the Blinkhorn family who were millers here from 1847 to 1922. It then became disused and derelict but R. J. Spain noted the name W. Weeks & Son of Maidstone on the machinery; they were the great local firm of mill machinery manufacturers whose wheels and gear were to be found in all the neighbourhood. Especially interesting is what was known as the Old Mill for here we find again mention of James Whatman, the famous paper manufacturer, who was granted the liberty in 1733 to "erect a new dwelling house and paper-mill." This had been an old fulling mill probably dating back to the Domesday survey but after its conversion to paper was finally taken over by

Balston, Finch Hollingworth & Co when Whatman retired in 1793. By 1850 it had switched to corn, but when Coles Finch visited it in 1933 it was utterly derelict and nothing now remains.

The Fulling Mill, Bollard's and Thurnham, the last named leased to Robert Blinkhorn, are only names on a map though Thurnham mill house still exists. But with Pole Mill we find James Whatman once again coming into the picture after it switched from fulling to paper, though for only a brief period before his retirement, after which Balston and the two Hollingworth brothers took over. Particularly interesting is the mention in an old deed of the adjoining tenter field where the fulled cloth was strung out on tenter hooks to dry in the fresh air. The site of this mill was submerged with the extension of the lake in Mote Park. However the next mill, the Turkey Mill, is perhaps the best known of all. At one time a fulling mill it was suggested that it was so named because of the red Turkey cloth brought here for fulling, there being rich veins of fuller's earth in the neighbourhood to supply the mill. However it is possible that it was once a corn-mill as 'Turkey Wheat' was the name given to maize or Indian corn in the sixteenth century. Turkey red as a dye for cloth was only introduced to France from Greece in 1740, reaching this country later still. Then in 1693 it was converted for the manufacture of paper and in 1719 Harris refers to the raw materials used for pulping, rags brought in by local people and also some from London, and the coarse brown paper made from old ropes, sails etcetera. In 1738 it was pulled down by the then owner Richard Harris and re-built, but on his death passed to his widow Ann who married James Whatman. By 1759 it was reckoned to be the largest paper mill in the country. In 1793 when James Whatman junior retired, Balston and the Hollingworths took it on, the last surviving Hollingworth brother dying in 1824 and leaving it to his sons. By 1899 it had passed to the nieces Mrs Pitt and Lady George Gordon-Lennox jointly and was still producing quality paper in the 1970s.

This brief survey of the Len mills has brought the waters of this little tributary to join through Mote Park the main stream of the Medway, but one great building is outstanding on its banks, a building which makes use of the river to encircle itself with a gleaming moat, creating the most enchanting setting for a Norman castle. There it stands, Leeds Castle, associated with so many English monarchs, centre for so much of English history to this day. To give it fair description and to record something of the critical scenes watched over by its stones requires another chapter.

CHAPTER EIGHT

Castles and Commerce

THE GREATEST of all the contrasts on this river of history and trade is between the sylvan charm of Leeds and the busy industrialism of the Medway Gap. There, brooding quietly in its lake surrounded by parkland and the young green of the spring foliaged trees, the gaunt stones of Leeds Castle have seen so many turbulent centuries. Yet what a place of beauty it is, this stately stronghold both fortress and dwelling-place, one of the favourite castles of our kings and queens throughout the Middle Ages, rising mysterious through autumnal mists or standing sheer in the sunshine.

The castle of Leeds stands on two little islands where the waters of the river Len fan out into a lake about four and a half miles south east of Maidstone. Close at hand the busy A20 swoops its way past the turning to Broomfield, the castle park-land fringes the road with stately trees, Leeds village lies about half a mile from the main highway. Visiting the site, it is easy to understand why it should have been selected as a stronghold by Saxon nobleman and Norman knight, with the two little islands only accessible by bridge or causeway.

After the Norman Conquest the ubiquitous Odo of Bayeux was given the title "Earl of Kent" and some two hundred manors scattered generally throughout the County, and Leeds was one of these. However there was probably only a primitive kind of stockade on the islands although one which would prove sufficiently defensible in case of an uprising by the indigenous English. It should not be forgotten that the Men of Kent and William I had made a treaty in 1066 before William entered London and the motto "Invicta" (unconquered), which emphasised that the Men of Kent had never actually been conquered by the Normans, would sum up very adequately the mood of the local inhabitants. Count Eustace of Bologne and Odo of Bayeux were particularly detested by them after the incident at Dover only fifteen years before when Eustace and his small bodyguard were set upon and driven out of the town. It was against such a background that the Norman nobles endeavoured to exert their authority by force of arms, and very soon the early primitive stockade forts and castles were re-built in stone. With the exile of the hated Odo some four years after the Domesday Survey the English saw Leeds Castle pass into the hands of Hamo de Crèvecoeur, a Norman baron whose son Robert began building a stone castle on the site that we see to-day, linked with the dry ground by drawbridge.

During the years of turmoil when Stephen and his cousin Matilda were disputing the throne the castle was in the thick of action, and again during the revolts of the barons against King John and Henry III. These rebellions eclipsed the de Crèvecoeurs, the castle passed to Roger de Leybourne, Warden of the Cinque Ports, and was then made over by his son William de Leybourne to King Edward I and his Queen, Eleanor of Castile. From this time onward, for some three hundred years, it was a favourite royal castle.

Edward I, that great and experienced castle builder, strengthened the Gate-house and added an Outer Bailey whose walls dropped sheer into the waters of the lake. This curtain wall was given flanking cover by towers built

Leeds Castle, serene within its lake. Described by Lord Conway as the loveliest castle in the world, it is open to the public and periods and days the castle is open can be obtained from the Estate Office. *Leeds Castle Foundation*

out at intervals, thus making the larger of the two islands very nearly impregnable. As a final retreat in case the Outer and Inner Baileys were captured a further drawbridge led to the smaller island on which was built a separate tower known as the Gloriette, mentioned already, and here defenders could make their final stand. There would not have been much comfort in the place in those days; such castles were designed primarily for defence. In the interesting guide to the castle, the author Lord Geoffrey-Lloyd makes reference to the fact that the King had intended giving Leeds to his Queen Eleanor as a dower. His affection for her is well known, stemming from the occasion when, on a Crusade, he had been struck at by an assassin armed with a poisoned dagger and she, with great presence of mind, sucked the poison from the wound. After her untimely death he established a chantry for her soul at Leeds; and on his later marriage to Margaret of France he granted it to her in turn as a dower-house.

The next strange thread in the pageant of history woven about this castle has to do with the haughty and rebellious Bartholomew de Badlesmere who had been granted the place by Edward II. Foolishly, in the absence of her husband, Lady de Badlesmere refused to entertain the Queen, Isabella, when she sought shelter there (possibly on her way from Dover); whereupon the King called forth an army and captured the castle, meeting out to de Badlesmere dire punishment for his lady's misdeeds. It has been suggested that this episode may well have been engineered by Edward to repossess himself of the castle in order to bestow it on his later favourites, the Despensers. Doubtless he was encouraged in his action by his Queen, the "she-wolf of France", who later turned against him, as is well known, contriving his death at Berkeley. Her son, Edward III, having put her well out of the way in Castle Rising in Norfolk, carried out many improvements in the Gloriette and in the royal apartments at Leeds.

Frequently during these perilous years successive kings held council meetings here at Leeds, and successive queens held the castle as a dower-house, among them Catherine of Valois whose marriage to Henry V was one of the stipulations of the peace treaty agreed after the victory at Agincourt. After the warrior king died so unexpectedly in 1422, the widowed queen dwelt here and possibly Owen Tudor was among her retinue. Certainly the Tudor rulers of later years, in particular Henry VIII, had a special affection for the place. It was this bluff and hearty monarch who made the most extensive improvements to the comfort of the castle while at the same time keeping the essentials of defence. Among other additions made at his command were the upper storey of the Gloriette, the enlargement of the bridge leading across from the main castle and an entirely new tower known as the Maidens' Tower, to house the Maids of Honour. We can imagine him withdrawing there from the affairs of state, perhaps enjoying music or playing his own elegant compositions, frequently also in the company of his closest confidants and advisers. It is very probable that Anne Boleyn came here with him, Catherine Howard is known to have spent much of her girlhood with the Culpepers at nearby Hollingbourne, Catherine Parr certainly came to Leeds. But after the death of Henry VIII the castle passed out of Royal hands. He intended that it should be granted to Sir Anthony St Leger whose loyal service as Lord Deputy in Ireland had brought unusual stability to our relationships with that troubled land, and the grant was actually made after his death, by his son King Edward VI.

There then followed a number of different owners until it came into the possession of Sir John Culpeper (later Lord Culpeper) who was one of King Charles I's most effective supporters in Parliament and who became Master of the Rolls. Not only this but he continued in loyal service to Charles II while he was in exile. There is an account in the castle guide of how the second Lord Culpeper gained the Governorship of Virginia for himself and how the estate then passed to his daughter Catherine who married the fifth Lord Fairfax. (The second Lord Fairfax, commander of the Parliamentary armies, had only daughters so the title passed to a cousin through whom the line descended). The Fairfax family fortunes ebbed and flowed, for nearly a hundred years there were difficulties over their American possesions. Then at last Leeds passed, again through the female line, to the Wykeham-Martins under whom a great work of restoration and improvement began in 1822. In 1926 it was bought by the Hon. Lady Baillie who set herself to make the castle the beautiful place it now is. She entertained widely in the thirties, the Duke of Windsor, the Duke and Duchess of Kent (Princess Marina) and many MPs being her guests; but in the early years of the Second World War it became a meeting place for members of the Allied Command, Lord Montgomery and Admiral Sir Bertram Ramsay who master-minded the Dunkirk evacuation being among those who gathered within these walls. Next it became a military hospital and Lady Baillie worked tirelessly to help wounded airmen back to health and strength.

It is easily understandable that when those critical years were passed she should wish the castle to continue to serve the nation. This was the origin of the Leeds Castle Foundation which now administers the estate; important meetings are still held here, scientists and eminent men consult on new discoveries, on occasion Heads of State discuss issues of national and international concern within these walls that have seen so much of England's history.

The Culpepper tomb, All Saints' Church, Hollingbourne. *Rev R. C. Bell* ▶

It seems appropriate now to leave this historic castle on the tributary river and pursue our way down to the greater Medway, for that Lord Culpeper of Leeds who was with Charles II in exile—and who, incidentally, was one of those behind his escape to France from Brighton in Nicholas Tettersell's collier-brig *Surprise*—would doubtless have seen and appreciated the way in which the assiduous Dutch made use of their waterways. Indeed discussions about the improvement of the banks and locks on the Medway might well have taken place within these castle walls. Only a very short distance away in All Saints' Church, Hollingbourne, is a lovely white marble recumbent figure of his wife, the Lady Elizabeth Culpeper who died in 1638. Also the church was well-known for the famous Culpeper altar-cloth which was worked by his four daughters while he was in exile with Charles II.

Making our way along the ancient track at the foot of the slope of the North Downs before joining the Medway again we come to the village of Boxley, with the remains of the famous Abbey close to the new motorway. Here once again we are in Wyatt country for there is a memorial to Sir Henry in the church which even mentions his faithful cat! St Mary and All Saints lies behind a tiny village green, probably dating from the thirteenth century and very likely the work of the monks from the Cistercian Abbey which was founded in 1146 by William of Ypres, Earl of Kent. It is extraordinary to find this isolated farming community only two miles from Maidstone and strange, too, to think that this was the only Cistercian Abbey in the whole of Kent for the followers of St Bernard were great tillers of the soil and normally kept flocks and herds and this fruitful county would provide ideal conditions for all husbandry. There is not very much left of the Abbey though the huge thirteenth century barn is an indication of the size and importance of the foundation. What does remain of walls and structures is largely incorporated in an eighteenth century house which also has some Tudor work in it as well, while other traces lie below the lawns and terraces. A careful inspection of the site in 1970-71 by the Kent Archaeological Society made it possible to confirm the lay-out of the various rooms of the Abbey and particularly the nave of the church whose walls, somewhat restored, enclosed a portion of the garden. It must have been in this church that the Rood of Grace was to be seen whose supernatural properties caused a flow of pilgrims to the spot in the later medieval times. It has been suggested that the great barn was once used as a guest-house to accommodate these many pilgrims. The Rood of Grace itself was a cross with a figure which was supposed to have miraculous powers; but at the time of the Dissolution, the Inspectors sent by Thomas Cromwell discovered various wires and other mechanism which would cause the eyes to roll and the lips to move as though about to speak. Such anyhow was their report but in fairness it must be added that Thomas Cromwell's agents were notoriously biased in their findings being "paid by results", and, at the

Wouldham Church from the river. *South Eastern Newspapers Limited*

dissolution of Boxley the Abbot received a life pension of £50—which surely would not have been paid to one guilty of a fraudulent trick; or perhaps Henry VIII, who was himself much given to practical jokes, appreciated the skill of the imposture. One of the most interesting features of the masonry unearthed during investigations was the considerable amount of carved chalk involved, for door jambs and openings in the church, for jambs in refectory, parlour and warming house (a large room adjoining the refectory probably for providing food and shelter for wayfarers), also in the nave arcades and the vaulting ribs of the chapter house. In the foundations of the north transept and presbytery many fragments of Roman roof-tile were to be found, also large pieces of box, or flue, tile and the distinctive Roman mortar. All this suggests that an earlier Roman building must have been on or near the site. Just outside the west end of the Abbey Church set in the ground was found a grave cover-stone of unusual shape with a rough cross on a rounded base. Most remarkable is the fact that it is Sarsen, very likely the sole example in Kent of the medieval use of this stone for such a purpose. Perhaps the reason would be the availability, as in the near neighbourhood were plenty of samples of megalithic tombs—and maybe this is one of the "Countless Stones" pressed into medieval use.

Another interesting feature in Boxley is Park House near the church, supposedly owned at one time by Alfred, Lord Tennyson. In any case he knew the place well and the little stream which rises in the grounds of the old Vicarage is supposed to have been an inspiration for the poem *The Brook*.

From Boxley down to the Medway is not far but we must not sweep away downstream before taking a final look at the paper industry, for, with Dartford, Maidstone was always the principal paper-making area of Kent and there are still a number of mills in operation to-day on the stretch of river between Maidstone and Rochester. To delve deep into the history of each one would be a mammoth undertaking and quite beyond the scope of this book which is focussed on the Medway river, but it is surely important to notice the main developments in the process and to take account of the three major features making this area so well suited for this manufacture, namely the river for bringing in rags and later the esparto grass and other necessary raw-materials; the proximity to London and simple communications with the capital; and above all the plentiful supply of good clean water. In the seventeenth and eighteenth centuries there was also the question of water-

Vatman making a sheet of paper. *H. R. Balston*

power to drive the machinery of the mills but by the early 1800s steam was in the offing.

A few interesting details come to light about the Maidstone area. The main group of older mills switched over to paper-making around 1670, that is to say Turkey, Upper Tovil, the two Ivy Mills and Loose. All the time they were up against stiff competition from abroad, principally France and the Low Countries, there was a great problem in obtaining sufficient rag and other raw material for pulping. However the outbreak of war in Europe in 1739 stimulated production in this country, and it was just about this time that James Whatman took over Turkey Mill.

It is instructive to look more closely at the history of this particular one as Whatman soon became important as a maker of the highest grade of white paper which, up to this time, had been imported by stationers and publishers. Indeed, by the end of the war against Spain in 1748 when trade was able to flow more freely again, the English paper makers, Whatman among them,

Rag sorting room. *H. R. Balston*

James Whatman the younger (left) and his wife Susannah, nee Bosanquet, who after his death continued to give assistance to William Balston in his new venture, bearing the Whatman name, at Springfield. *H. R. Balston*

had captured the bulk of the market. Dr A. H. Shorter in his *Paper-making in the British Isles* reveals that by the middle of the eighteenth century Kent was in the lead in the number of mills making high quality paper; and Turkey Mill under James Whatman and his son, James the younger, was the best. It was to the latter that Hasted referred when he said that he (Whatman) "with infinite pains and expense has brought his manufacturing of writing paper, for no other is made here, to a degree of perfection superior to most in this Kingdom." Thomas Balson in his *James Whatman, Father and Son* gives us an interesting account of how the business developed, James the younger becoming increasingly successful, being High Sheriff of Kent in 1767, and able to buy the adjoining estate of Vinters in 1783. Meanwhile as he had no son by his first marriage, he had taken William Balston as an apprentice and he soon showed great aptitude for the work. James, however, had a son by his second wife, Susanna Bosanquet; then the family came to Vinters and Balston joined them there. By this time Whatman paper was becoming widely known, and had even built up quite a considerable export business to America. As a result of this, and wise investment, James was able to buy further estates; but unhappily when only forty-eight years old he suffered a slight stroke and, leaving William Balston in charge, went off to Margate to recuperate. After this illness and with increasing labour unrest both in this country and on the

Beam of the mill's Boulton and Watt beam engine, still preserved at Springfield. *H. R. Balston*

continent, it is easy to appreciate why he decided to sell Turkey Mill in 1793 to two brothers, Thomas and Finch Hollingworth. William Balston went into partnership with them to provide the expert knowledge which he had acquired in his twenty-three years with the firm. Still living at Vinters and taking a keen interest in the success of the partnership James helped with advice until his death in 1798.

For eleven years William Balston was the technical director of the firm, but as Thomas Balston mentions in his book *William Balston paper-maker*, he now determined to make a move from Turkey Mill to Springfield on the main river where there were essential supplies of the pure spring water necessary for making the highest quality of good white paper. These springs were supposed to rise from a great depth but it is now known that they come from the "buried channel" of the river. The partnership with the Hollingworths was dissolved and work began on the new site, which had the advantage of not being cramped like the earlier mills by the need to be built across a narrow river-valley to take advantage of water-power and the draughts of air up and down stream. The frontage of the great mill extended for some 440 feet parallel to the Medway and from the very first he was intent upon using steam as his power; as Thomas Balson says, "he is believed to have been the pioneer in the sole use of steam". Consulting with John Rennie, the famous engineer and bridge-builder, and with Boulton, Watt & Co, he presently decided on a 36 h.p. beam engine which was duly brought up the Medway and installed, there to work for the next ninety years. The beam is still preserved at Springfield. However he did not allow his works to become fully mechanised for, as Thomas Balston says, "he continued to make many grades of printing papers in rather desperate competition with the machines, but gradually he concentrated on writing and drawing papers stronger and more durable than the machines proved able to produce. It was by these papers that the Whatman watermark became famous throughout the world".

All this while Chairman of the Master Paper-Makers of Kent, also at times being Chairman of the even larger group of Master Paper-Makers of England, Balston's new venture was hindered by the high cost of rags and the uncertainty of trade during the long years of war with France.

However, though hampered by financial difficulties, and eventually having to go into partnership with Bosanquet and Gaussen he managed to carry on until at last the tide turned in the late 1820s and from then onward the firm continued to prosper and is still among the largest in the Maidstone area.

Exterior of building, both floors of which were used for rag sorting. *H. R. Balston*

Springfield Mill. *H. R. Balston*

Now, well over a century later, the whole scene is transformed with only Hayle Mill and Springfield producing specialised papers, but the industry otherwise dominated by the huge Reed mills at New Hythe and such concerns as Townsend Hook at Snodland.

Reference to New Hythe and the huge works of the Reed Group extending over more than 500 acres and importing via the river many hundreds of tons of wood pulp, board, coal, and china clay as size provides a staggering contrast with earlier centuries. When the navigation was remodelled and Reed's established their mills with the loading berths and gantries, the meandering shallows of what is known as "Burham Old River" were clearly useless for the increased traffic. The "Middle Cut" was therefore constructed to link up with the "Upper Cut" leading through to Aylesford and Allington Lock. However, in the early days New Hythe was part of East Malling and in the fourteenth century appears to have been a centre for the loading and trans-shipment of timber. Then, in Tudor times, a family of wool-merchants, the Celys, were carrying on a considerable trade across the channel and reference is made in some of their documents published by the Royal Historical Society to the names of ships involved. There is the *Mary of Malling*, and a little later the *Thomas of Newhythe*; also in another document the *Barbara of Malling* is mentioned. Obviously these ships must have been of reasonable size (up to about 60 tons), equivalent indeed to the hoys owned and trading to and from Maidstone; a century or so later we find reference made to a certain George Westerly who left a share in his hoy the *George* to his daughter in his will proved in 1689. It is likely also that ships were built or repaired at New Hythe about this time as there is a reference in the will of James Maylin, a shipwright to the "Garden Wharfe or Keye and the ferry yearde".

Snodland Paper Mill fire, 12th August 1906.

Down the river from New Hythe the waters tend to wind to and fro with here and there a stretch of cement wharf or disused works, which appeared to one informant "like deserted castles, quite eerie to walk about in", and on the east side a reed-fringed island where an old channel used to flow. A little way inland there were the remains of the Roman villa at Eccles, remains so extensive that they indicated the luxurious residence of a very civilised landowner whose estate would have been far-spreading, possibly including quarries as well as farms. Here along this stretch down as far as Snodland and Burham the mayor and jurats (aldermen) of Maidstone used to make their cheerful and ceremonial progress once a year in Tudor times, with full pageantry, to confirm piscatorial rights granted them by Queen Elizabeth I, and also brand all swans on the river as theirs for which they had authority and a special swan-mark.

At Snodland just where the river makes a big loop there is the possible crossing of the Pilgrims' Way, though the hard bottom to the river is really caused not by a made ford but by a natural outcrop of greensand rock. Here, in what is known as Church Field, C. Roach Smith noted in 1844* that tesserae of Roman pavements, fragments of roof and flue tiles were found and also remains of walls and a floor. In 1964 a rescue excavation was undertaken when the South Eastern Gas Board was doing clearing operations and work was also being done in the grounds of the Lead Wool Co Ltd., and traces of rooms, small fragments of red and green wall-plaster, a hypocaust and a plunge bath

*A report on this was given in *Arch. Cant. LXXXII.*

or water-tank were discovered as well as a corridor and an apsidal structure. So far as can be determined the remains suggest at least two buildings both with mosaic floors and one some 31 feet in width. Most of the potsherds discovered were of the late second to mid-third century A.D., though some were after the latter date; but as so few parts of the building remained intact it is almost impossible to suggest the kind of occupation. However it is clear that the site was of some size, stretching for several hundred feet along the west bank of the Medway which would have given it good and easy communication with nearby Rochester.

It was at Snodland, too, that the disastrous paper-mill fire of 1906 occurred which completely destroyed Townsend Hook's works, the damage being estimated at £150,000, when showers of cancelled postal orders sent there for pulping flew about the fields like charred confetti to the excitement of the local children. However the Insurance cover was sufficient to assist in the re-building of the mill and after about two years it was again trading profitably.

Over the other side of the river the furthest up-stream cement works were situated, these belonging to the Burham Brick Cement and Lime Company. As with all such companies they had their own fleet of spritsail barges, those very typical vessels of our river, with their bluff bows, swelling tan mains'l and tops'l, and small mizzen aft; like all lime and cement-carriers they were maintained in tip-top condition. The reason for this is obvious when it is remembered that in the early days much of the lime was shipped direct from

Peters Brothers' Wouldham Hall Cement Works, showing the remains of wooden loading chutes. The works was badly situated for transport, so cement was loaded on lighters, ferried across the Medway and thence taken by cart to Snodland station. This photograph was taken from motor barge *Olive May* in December 1965. *Patricia O'Driscoll*

the kilns so that it was in the form of "quick lime", and any moisture would start it slaking and generate enough heat to char some of the woodwork or even start up a disastrous fire. All the Burham barges were small as the river runs very shallow up at that point; and with a grey rail, green transom and a big white B on the tops'l they looked very handsome.

Coke was the main fuel used for lime burning, so most of the barges taking a freight round to the Thames would work up to one of the gas works after discharging their lime. From Tudor times onward every village between Maidstone and Rochester would have its wharf, and many of the supplies for the rather isolated hamlets would come up the river as return loads.

This point on the river has always been the traditional division between the upper and lower Medway administration, the position marked by what is known as the Hawkwood Stone on the Burham bank opposite Snodland. And here, too, is a most trickly place for navigation as, at low spring tides, the river very nearly dries out. The flat spritsail barge, the only keel provided by her lee-boards, was obviously the ideal kind of craft for such waters where she could take the bottom without harm and remain upright.

A glance at the chart will show the complications of making passage up or down the river. Even with the advantages of the Lower and Middle Cuts and, in later years, being shoved along by an auxiliary engine, the stretch up from Wouldham to New Hythe was a tedious one. Tugs and barges, auxiliary craft and lighters would be working their tides; and, when darkness fell, the whole business became even more tricky. One who knows these waters well described how, above Rochester Bridge, it was very difficult to see anything at all after dark, the position being made even worse by the shadows of trees. By day barges would raise their gear as soon as they were above the bridge so that craft coming down would spot them from a distance. By night special mast-head lights would be shown from a "light iron". Those who came in on sea-going barges used to refer to the regular users of the upper Medway as "the reed sparrows".

During the next couple of miles the river begins to widen, the tidal flow becomes more pronounced, and tugs and barges glide along between some quite pleasant stretches of country although the ground tends to be pock-marked with old disused chalk-pits, some of them utilised as rubbish-dumps. But very soon the large cement works belch smoke into the air, there are quarries and chalk excavations on the hill slopes behind Halling and at Holborough Hill more excavations. Those being carried out at the Associated Portland Cement Manufacturing Company's works at Holborough revealed a

The "knocker-on" using the club to drive the sharp hooks of the lifting chains into bales of pulp. The chains were then hooked on to the crane unloading at New Hythe. *Patricia O'Driscoll*

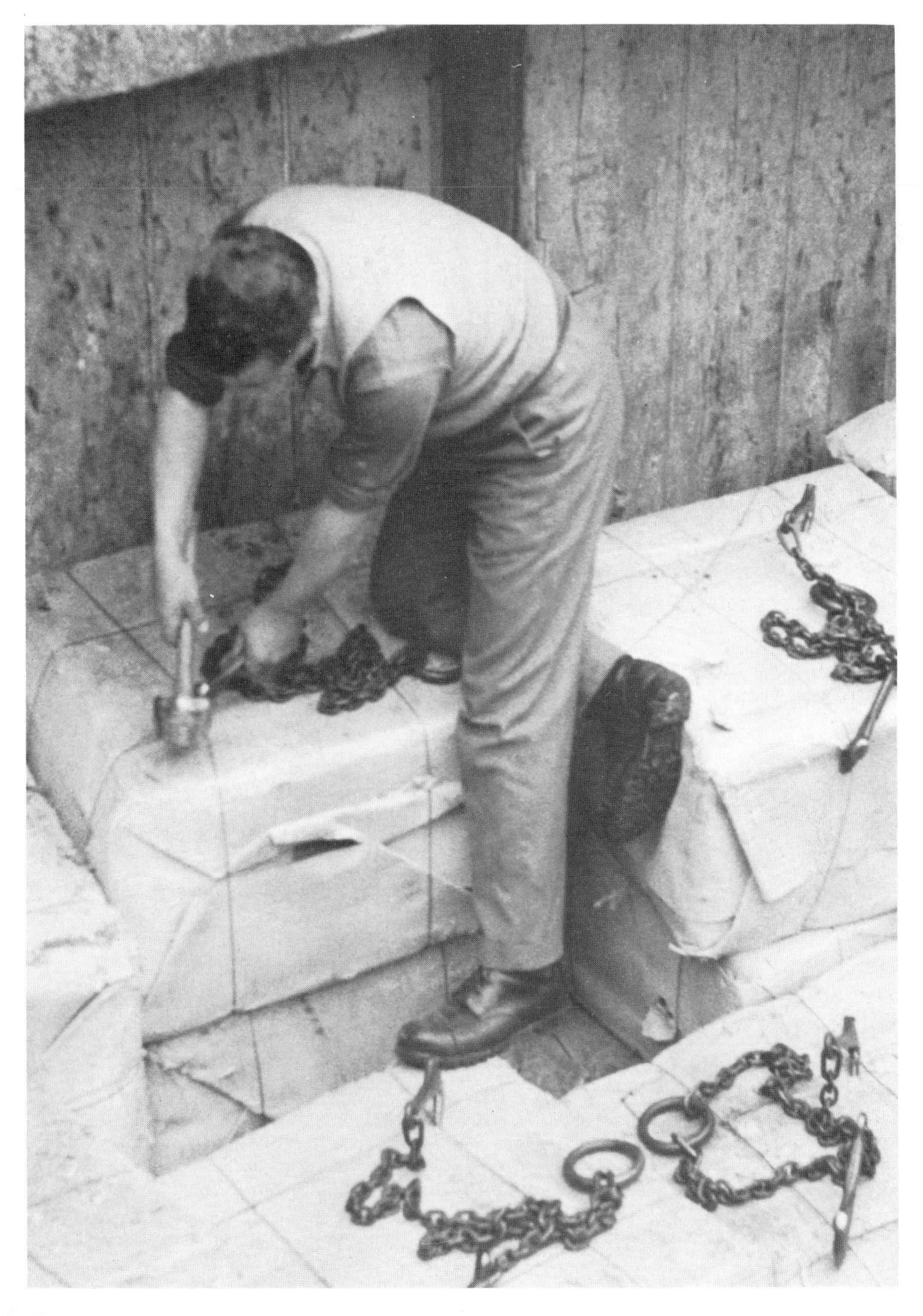

number of graves, which proved to be of Anglo-Saxon date, around the seventh century. Detailed examination as far as was possible showed that the site was an Anglo-Saxon or Jutish cemetery not far from the Roman tumulus known as Holborough Knob, but the full extent was impossible to determine as other graves had probably been lost through the quarrying. However thirty-nine were located, in nine of which there were finds, among other items an interesting iron inlaid spearhead, four shield bosses, open work and bird-headed buckles, an iron chain pot-hanger, pottery and a small whet-stone. In sharp contrast to such a historical site, only a few miles away the M2 motorway bridge straddles the countryside downstream, its high concrete piers rising majestically and vehicles tearing along in droves above peaceful fields and marshes. Amid all this the ancient church at the end of Wouldham village seems an outpost of quietness, where lies buried the purser of H.M.S. *Victory*, Walter Burke, who, with Captain Hardy, was supporting Lord Nelson when he died at the Battle of Trafalgar; on Trafalgar Day there is a tradition that the local people lay flowers on his grave. A short distance further on there is an old farm-house named Starkey Castle, and also, close to the Shoulder of Mutton Wood, a mound sometimes known as Wouldham Castle. The Lower Medway Archaeological Group carried out an investigation in 1968 but though foundations of chalk rubble were located, the shape of these, and the absence of any sherds older than eighteenth century seemed to indicate nothing more than a mill-mound—the base for a windmill. At Cuxton, on the other side of the river, was the site of Whorne's Place where once a Tudor mansion stood—the home of the Lord Mayor of London; now new buildings and development creep up onto the sky line among the trees, defacing a lovely fold of country near to the main railway line at the summit of the Chatham Bank.

Now our river, full and wide, sweeps down towards the city of Rochester, with Strood and Frindsbury on the far side and the great castle and cathedral gazing down benignly over the maze of buildings that climb the slopes and cluster near the waterfront.

Whatman ream stamp of 1770. *H. R. Balston*

CHAPTER NINE

City and Bridge

THE TOWERING concrete piers of the M2 motorway viaduct provide a boundary for the clambering outskirts of Rochester, the factory and other buildings of Strood. Down by the riverside, to the south west and dwarfed by the tall pillars, the Wouldham marshes extend on the one bank, on the other the railway-line and road from Maidstone skirt the water's edge. Cement works, factories, brickfields are scattered about, but there are also farms and wide spaces. However, downstream of the bridge the contrast is considerable. On the Rochester bank the Medway yacht basin provides secluded mooring space for glass-fibre hulls and traditional wooden-built vessels and a sight reminiscent of earlier years, an old paddle-steamer on which enthusiasts have been busy, trying to bring her back to her former state of seaworthiness. Very soon comes a built up area with huge factory sheds along the Esplanade, then the Cathedral and the towering castle with grassy lawns stretching down to the waterside and the pier. A desolate space on the other bank is sandwiched between the two separate railway tracks, one linking Strood to Maidstone and the other Rochester to London, which here run more or less parallel though at different levels. This space leads in to the clustered buildings, shops, warehouses and works of Strood. The river itself, gathering strength, suddenly widens, the waters glisten as they swirl along Tower reach and become compressed again into a narrow defile as they shoot under the twin road and rail bridges. Forty foot of headroom sounds a lot, but that is at low water and at spring tides. Normally there is nothing like that amount and in any case one has to have the benefit of the tide to work through the spans where the water pours through like a mill-race. With an 18 foot difference between high and low water the current is something to be reckoned with especially when lighters, barges or perhaps big ocean going vessels are manoevring, swinging athwart one's course.

Like every town situated at the crossing of a river, the history of Rochester and its bridge are very closely linked; but with this particular bridge there are unique features as will be explained later. A settlement of great importance was certainly here in pre-Roman days and there were ancient crossings at several places in the Medway Gap. However these were all concerned with the Pilgrims' Way or North Downs Way, both of which were meandering tracks dating from very early times. For the Romans, Durobrivae (Rochester) was the next main town along Watling Street after Durovernum Cantiacorum (Canterbury) so a crossing of the river, presumably by a wooden bridge, would undoubtedly have been effected. The Roman alignment of Rochester and Strood High Street is definite and the bridge constructed in 1865 by Cubitt followed this line. Of course all Romano-British towns were extraordinarily small to our eyes. Canterbury for example, consisting of some 130 acres, was larger than normal and Rochester would have been appreciably smaller than this. Nonetheless it was an important town, with the customary stone protecting wall and guarded gates. In an excavation carried out in the 1960s some interesting facts about one section of the Roman wall near the south east corner appeared. The masonry seems to have been bedded on a layer of concrete fifteen inches thick, and this concrete raft was about eight feet wide. To increase the strength of the foundations the facing blocks of ragstone were inset by a foot at intervals of about every six courses until the wall was 4' 6" in width. The core of the wall was found to be of ragstone rubble well mixed in with a mortar of a hard gritty brown colour. Much of the Roman wall has been traced, some of it under later medieval walls, some of it in the castle walls.

After the Roman departure and the establishment of the Saxon (West Kent) or Jutish (East Kent) kingdoms Rochester has been suggested as the capital of a northern sub-kingdom and Canterbury of the south. How much truth there is in this is uncertain; but it is definite that following St Augustine's

Rochester Castle and Cathedral. *Clive Lawford*

The medieval stone bridge at Rochester, after the railings had been replaced by a stone balustrade, from an old print. *Kent County Library*

mission and his appointment as Archbishop of Canterbury in 597, a second diocese was created in 604 with its cathedral at Rochester, Ethelbert King of Kent setting aside the land known as Priestfield for the purpose. Justus, one of St Augustine's followers, was the first bishop, being translated to Canterbury in 624. Thus Kent became the only English county divided between two sees.

It is astonishing to think of these early beginnings when we gaze at the wharves and shipbuilding yards of modern Rochester, but over all frowns the great keep of the Norman castle 125 feet high, a reminder of the constant guard that has been maintained throughout the ages over the river crossing. Here we come to the next great name in the history of the city, Bishop Gundulf. Exactly when he undertook the fortification of the castle is not clear, but there was certainly some kind of a stronghold that was in the possession of supporters of Duke Robert who were duly besieged and overwhelmed by William Rufus in 1088. The Bishop must have carried on with his building, parts of his wall are up against and partly on top of the Roman wall; other parts are built on a bank of chalk rubble which may perhaps have been a section of earlier earthworks. However he was not only at work on the castle for he had also built the major portion of the cathedral within the first seven years of his consecration. The intention was undoubtedly to build a splendid cathedral church dedicated to St Andrew but over and over again it was damaged, first in the Barons' Wars and much later by Cromwellian soldiery who used part of it as a carpenters' and builders' store, and another as an eating-place. Only the fine West Front and the Chapter House of the present fabric are twelfth century as a terrible fire swept the city in 1137; therefore most of the cathedral is the result of later re-building, but the west door is a beautiful example of Norman work. There are some interesting monuments inside, one to Bishop Walter de Merton, founder of the Oxford College of that name, also a brass to Charles Dickens, so much associated with this city. As well there is the reputed tomb of St William of Perth, a charitable baker who, as Teignmouth Shore in *Kent* says, on pilgrimage to the Holy Land, was "spoiled both of his money and his life" by his servant in 1201. His tomb became a place of pilgrimage rather like that of Becket at Canterbury. Gundulf also reorganised the attached Priory of St Andrew, arranging that as well as rents, pensions and tithes the monks should also have numerous manors, including among others Wouldham, Frindsbury and Southfleet. When Henry I confirmed these arrangements he added many churches as well, some as far as Stourmouth; so it will be realised that this Priory was very

Sailing barge hoisting her gear having just shot Rochester bridge. The extra man forrard is the huffler, taken on to assist her through. A fine view of the cathedral and castle in the background. *Alan Cordell*

wealthy. However as it was the next door to the castle constant damage was sustained during the various attacks, but the monks were generously recompensed and when finally the Priory was surrendered at the Dissolution the list of lands and properties in its ownership was found to be very extensive.

The castle meanwhile was further added to and strengthened by successive builders, among them Archbishop William de Corbeuil of Canterbury; there it stood massive and frowning, well supplied with dungeons, keeping watch and ward over the bridge, its great twelve foot thick walls rising into the air. One thing that makes it most unusual is that three corner towers are square and one, the south eastern, is rounded. This was the result of a siege by the troops of King John after the signing of the Magna Carta; for when the King appealed to the Pope for support in his stand against the barons and was down at Dover waiting for some expected reinforcements, the seneschal of the castle permitted it to be occupied by rebel barons. As soon as he heard this dire news the King returned to lay siege to the place, and finding other means of storming it fruitless, undermined the south eastern tower. Brushwood was packed into the excavation, the whole lot was fired, the earth cracked and gave way in the heat and down came the tower. We can well imagine the resultant furious onslaught which brought victory to the King; and when comparative calm descended on the country and re-building could begin under Henry III the fashion in towers had changed to the rounded variety—less easy to undermine.

From the keep there is a tremendous view over the sweep of the river as it makes its hairpin bend heading for Chatham Ness; also we look down over the bridge and imagine the great medieval stone structure which was erected in 1383 in place of the previous timber one which had had such a parlous time of it in the warlike years of the Normans and Angevins. Hasted goes into great detail about the early bridge, its ten spans and nine piers, the upkeep of which was apportioned out among various neighbouring parishes or the inhabitants of the local Hundreds. The net was spread far and wide—to Teston for example on the one hand, to Hoo on the other, but even this was not enough to ensure any consistent repair work. On several occasions during the various struggles between the Barons and the Crown during the reigns of King John and Henry III efforts were made to interfere with the passage of armies by setting fire to it. In 1281, after a prolonged freeze up, when the river was in spate through melting ice and snow, great ice-floes cannoning into the piers caused such damage that for a number of years the crossing had to be by boat. Some half-hearted efforts at repair patched it up in due course, but when Edward III was preparing his French campaigns in the Hundred Years' War he found this essential crossing, on the Dover road, Watling Street, quite unfit for the passage of troops. He was not the person to tolerate this so an inquiry was instituted to find out the reasons for the failure to repair.

A distant view of Rochester bridge, castle and cathedral, with wharves and warehouses in the foreground. *Clive Lawford*

For nearly forty years after the capture of Calais in 1347 first one and then another noble was ordered to effect repairs. Finally, in 1382, with the wretched thing again ruinous and impassable, Sir John de Cobham, of Cooling Castle, and Sir Robert Knolles, one of Edward III's commanders in the field, were commissioned to overhaul or renew it. Providing much of the material themselves and at their own cost, these two employed the master mason Yevele who had earlier built Queenborough Castle, and set about an entirely new structure some one hundred yards upstream from the old. Great elm piles were driven in clusters into the stream bed to form caissons which were then packed tight with chalk. Over this came a platform of Kentish ragstone and the masonry of the arches thus had a good solid foundation. The work was not finally completed till 1392 but we get an idea of how competent and thorough was the building by the fact that it lasted on, through storm and shine till 1856, and was only demoslished then because the huge foundation-caissons were causing mud-banks and bars to form, thus hampering navigation. Much of the masonry from this old bridge went into the building of the esplanade.

One of the most peculiar features of this bridge has not yet been mentioned, namely that it is a considerable land-owner. This came about through Cobham and Knolles gaining permission from the King to invest in real estate in order to defray expenses, so that land is owned on behalf of the Bridge Trust in the Isle of Grain, Tilbury, and the Hundred of Hoo and many

Rochester's busy wharves and shipyards, taken from near the Medway College of Design.
Clive Lawford

other places amounting in all to over two thousand acres. By letters patent of 1398 the owners of lands contributing to the repair of the bridge were authorised to form themselves into a community to elect Wardens annually to administer affairs and an Act of Henry V in 1420 granted them a Common Seal as "Wardens and Commonalty of the new bridge of Rochester." However in course of time it became difficult to identify the persons entitled to vote so a new Constitution for the Court of Wardens and Assistants was laid down by the Rochester Bridge Act of 1908 whereby it was enacted that the Court should consist of six members nominated by the County Council, two each nominated by Maidstone and Gillingham Borough Councils, four by Medway Borough Council and three from the Medway Ports Authority.

By 1914 the 1856 bridge was becoming too much of an obstruction to traffic up and down river owing to the fact that the railway bridges were next to it so the Wardens re-built with the present bow-girders; one of the railway bridges was purchased and converted into a road bridge—it was opened to traffic in 1970. It is interesting to note that except for a tax levied by Elizabeth I over the whole county, and a few occasions when the bridge has been damaged and ferries have been substituted and empowered to make a charge, the bridge has not cost the public anything at all since the foundation of the Trust. It is appropriate, too, that the Court should hold its meetings in the old Bridge Chapel which was built in 1387 by Sir John de Cobham. Such little chapels were very frequently connected with medieval bridges; but this one was suppressed as a chantry in 1549 and used in various ways, among others as an eating house, gradually becoming ruinous. It was then restored in 1937 and put to its present use as an assembly hall and museum, with the Bridge Chambers where all the records are kept alongside it.

Mention of the Esplanade brings to mind the wonderful sight of a huge Empire flying-boat moored in midstream a little distance above Rochester Bridge. Here indeed was one of the greatest contrasts of all, the Norman Keep and the flying machine. The story of how this came about is interesting and typical of the originality and drive always in the past associated with famous English companies, qualities which we hope and believe are still strong in this country.

The three brothers Horace, Eustace and Oswald Short had an engineering background and after leaving school had many and various experiences, Horace having a spell as a captive and a god in the hands of cannibals before

Short flying boat *Canopus* moored off the Esplanade, Rochester. *J. M. Preston*

The loop of river from Limehouse Reach to Chatham Reach—a panoramic view with the hospital in the foreground. Chatham is in the right background. *Clive Lawford*

managing a mine in South America, Eustace becoming involved with gas balloons, and Oswald joining Wilbur and Orville Wright in their experiments with flying machines. As a result the three Short brothers set up business underneath some railway arches at Battersea, London, as aircraft manufacturers. This made them the world's first aeroplane makers.

In the course of the few years between 1908 and the First World War they moved to Eastchurch in the Isle of Sheppey, building their first factory here of corrugated iron. Numerous experimental planes were developed, naval lieutenants were taught how to handle controls, one of whom made the first landing of an aircraft on water in Sheerness harbour, the machine having buoyancy bags lashed to skids beneath the fuselage to keep it up. This of course was the beginning of Short's connection with amphibian aircraft; but Eastchurch was unsuitable for such development, so Tower Field, Rochester, was acquired and a new works erected facing onto the river just above the bridge.

Throughout the war years they were hard at work developing torpedo-carrying aircraft, while Eustace concentrated on blimps and observation balloons; but this was only the prelude to rapid expansion after the Armistice. By 1920 they had the first all-metal aircraft in the air, and by 1924 the first all-metal seaplane. With true initiative they refused to lose their skilled work-force in the tough years of recession in 1923 and 1924, going in for every sort of manufacture from light-weight bus bodies for Tillings and the London General Bus Co. to prams. Sailing barges were built too, among them the

Lord Haigh in 1930, the last sailing barge built on the Medway. Presently aeroplane work picked up again with such famous designs as the Singapore flying boat, the great Empire flying boats used so widely by Imperial Airways on their world-wide services, and later the Stirling bomber. The Sunderland flying boat was their final development but after the Second World War production at Rochester was found to be too costly by comparison with other factories elsewhere (possibly because of the cost of labour); so, sadly, the works were closed in 1948. The firm of Short and Harland continued their operations from Belfast. A full account of the firm and its work can be found In J. M. Preston's interesting book *A Short History*.

It would be impossible, as with the many industries higher up the river, to go into specific detail of the ship-building yards, the manufactures of every kind that are carried on round about Rochester Bridge. But before we go across to the other side of the river to investigate there, we must not forget the other interesting associations with Rochester, for this has been the place through which, over many centuries, everyone travelling to Dover or the continent has passed. King Charles I came this way in haste on his way to greet his future Queen Henrietta Maria at Dover, stopping for a meal with the Dean where the naval architect Phineas Pett also attended upon him. Then, on their return towards London together, Charles and the Queen received a "noble and most hearty welcome"* from the Mayor, magistrates and citizens; and, as they rode on their way "a brave volley of shot and great ordnance was delivered from the shippes which lay upon the river."

The *George Inn* in the High Street must have welcomed many visitors in its time but is built above a far more ancient cellar of the fifteenth century which must have belonged to a house of great eminence and style. Mr Geroge Payne, who did so much restoration work in the city, explored it, discovering that it was a huge crypt-like room fifty-four feet in length by sixteen feet eight inches in width, having a vaulted ceiling decorated with ornate ribbing.

Another famous foundation here, associated with the Cathedral, is the school which at the Dissolution was re-founded as the King's School. It still makes use of some of the old buildings but has spread into other parts of the town as well, among others to the fine red-brick Elizabethan house with the Flemish gables which is known as Restoration House by reason of the fact that Charles II is supposed to have stayed here on his triumphant progress from Dover to London on his return from exile in 1660. There is yet another of these fine sixteenth century town houses, Eastgate House, which is now the City museum, and which contains many items connected with Charles Dickens and the years he spent at Gad's Hill. The gilded weather-vane of a ship which glints proudly above the seventeenth century Guildhall reminds us that this city is essentially a port, the hub of trade which spreads out in all directions, to Scandinavia, to ports in the Mediterranean, and to coastwise traffic of every

*From a pamphlet "A True Discourse" quoted by Margaret Toynbee in *Arch. Cant.* 1955.

Sailing barge *Ardeer*. The graceful lines of these sturdy craft can be appreciated from this fine photograph. *Alan Cordell*

kind. Great names in naval history too are connected with the port of Rochester for the Corn Exchange built in 1706 was the work of Sir Cloudesley Shovell; Lord Nelson himself has the most intimate association with the place, though even more so with Chatham where he joined his first ship, the *Raisonnable* at the tender age of twelve in 1771. He is supposed to have stayed at Rochester in 1805 on his way to inspect the fleet then lying in the Downs.

The sniff of salt water is in our nostrils as we think of the great Chatham naval base just round the loop of the river but there are still a number of items peculiar to Rochester that we should not omit. From the very early times apart from the trade upon the river, there was also a great deal made of what was contained in it. A large and flourishing fishing industry was carried on below Rochester and in the creeks of the Lower Medway, the whole controlled by an Admiralty court under the Mayor of the city. It was recorded that very fine and large smelts* were taken as well as soles, dabs and flounders; but the most famous of all were the oysters. Although perhaps not rivalling the Whitstable

*After not being seen for years smelts have returned to the Medway in the last eighteen months or so.

KK9032

"natives", oysters from the Medway were regarded as a great delicacy. They were taken to the Billingsgate fish market as soon as London began to increase in size but in the seventeenth century were even exported to Holland. In the eighteenth century this oyster fishery became so famous, and profitable for the city, that its operations were governed by a special Act and the most stringent regulations were laid down as to the time of year when fishing might be undertaken, the fact that only oysters over eighteen months old might be dredged and so on. This oyster fishery remained a very profitable undertaking right through to the middle of the nineteenth century.

Strood on the other side of the river was especially a fishing town with a fish market near Strood Hard. There was quite a large fleet of bawleys* based there which used to set forth and sometimes spend a whole week shrimping or trawling further down the river. Other smaller boats would work upstream even as far as Aylesford and in 1980 boats have gone up smelt fishing as far as Halling. It is interesting to think of this great trade in river-fishing in view of the miles of river now used almost entirely for the sport of angling in the higher reaches up beyond Tonbridge.

Before we go over the bridge to Strood mention ought to be made of another very famous company whose prancing Kentish horse motif was known so widely all over the country; and this was a particularly appropriate undertaking, too, in view of the great agricultural connection with the river, and the fact that Kent is such an outstanding agricultural county. I refer of course to one of the best known of the Rochester engineering firms, Aveling and Porter. Founded in the 1890s by a Ruckinge farmer, Thomas Aveling, it was not long before steam traction engines were becoming familiar sights, first standing at either side of a field and drawing a plough to and fro across it, then as road locomotives either for drawing carts of produce or later still as road rollers. It is still a nostalgic sight when at some county show there is a rally of steam traction engines and it is quite a thrill to see the proud horse of Kent gleaming on some marvellously reconditioned and polished engine. It was firms of this calibre that made the city of Rochester famed as a centre of engineering prowess, but there were numbers of other undertakings as will be seen in the next chapter, though only the briefest mention can be made. Through them all runs the thread of communication spun by our river, the easy import of raw materials and the ready market for goods of all kinds in the great city of London.

A final adjustment for an Invicta (Aveling and Porter) steam roller at Quexpo Steam Engine Rally. *Photograph by Anthony Bryan, reproduced by kind permission of Quexpo*

*Bawley—coastal fishing boats or oyster dredgers peculiar to the Thames Estuary area from Harwich to Whitstable.

CHAPTER TEN

Strood, Gad's Hill and Acorn Wharf

THE BIOGRAPHY of the river has reached its most exciting and important phase when, having left behind the winding streams passing the lovely orchards, the hop gardens and the picturesque oasts and also the later mercantile reaches between the county town and the city of Rochester, the sniff of the sea and the ocean-going ships speak of the great waters of the world. Here, passing through the years, hoys and later barges with gear partly lowered have shot Rochester Bridge, ship building and repair have been major industries and most ingenious engineering has been directed to the efficient movement of goods from inland. Yet only some one hundred and eighty years ago Rochester was without industry, mostly known for its riverside walks, the threads of history thickly woven around this, one of our earliest cities.

Over the other side of the bridge the fishing port of Strood had also a most ancient foundation, the Hospital of St Mary established by Bishop Gilbert de Glanville in around 1192. These hospitals were partly to give refreshment to passing wayfarers, particularly those going on pilgrimage, but they also played a big part in caring for elderly and sick people, and the poor. There were more than forty of them in Kent, the greater number lying along the course of Watling Street, Canterbury having no less than ten. Under the original Charter this St Mary's was to have a Master, two priests, two deacons and two sub-deacons and, as with Rochester Priory, the funds for the upkeep and maintenance were to be provided by tithes from surrounding villages and various churches. This was a most unhappy arrangement as the monks from the Priory reckoned these tithes to have been robbed from their endowment and there was everlasting friction between the two foundations until in the end King Henry VIII ordered the Hospital to be handed over to the priory with all its property.

Before we turn the corner down into the next reach of the river there are many details about Strood and Frindsbury which it would be wrong not to mention. In particular we must look a little more closely into the process of making cement for there was a big works at Strood Dock which was very typical of the Cement industry. Basically what was needed for cement was chalk and mud or clay. These ingredients were mixed together with water into a milk-like liquid which was allowed to settle in dug-out "pans". When evaporation had caused this mixture to become a kind of sticky sludge it would be scooped out, wheeled off to the beehive-shaped kilns and there baked after which the resultant slag would be ground to a fine powder. Edwin Harris in *The Riverside* goes into considerable detail of the works by Strood Dock and the various processes, but this very simplified account will at least go to show that the two main ingredients were in plentiful supply in the Medway Gap. Chalk was very simply quarried from the steep chalk cliffs, the mud was readily obtainable from the marshes down below Gillingham, the barges being allowed to drift in at high tide and ground when the water level fell. The bargemen would then clamber over the side to dig out what they required, float on the next tide and sail up to the works. This was one of the reasons for the great fleet of barges operating in the Medway, but there were also many other circumstances that led to the development of this particular craft, which we will look at later. Following the same fairly primitive procedure there were some eleven cement works in operation by the 1860s, at Snodland, Cuxton, Burham, Wouldham, Halling, Borstal and Upnor as well as at Frindsbury; and all the product of these works would be shifted by water, each firm having its own fleet of spritsail barges.

Mention of one concern, the Medway Cement Works, Strood, which had a contract to supply the French Government with cement reminds us that its

Chalk and mud for cement in the 19th century. *J. M. Preston*

Strood basin — oil seed was imported through here. *J. M. Preston*

works were just to the north east of the Canal basin. This Canal was a most interesting feature, an original scheme linked with the increasing use of the Medway as a waterway for the transport of goods. Of course, as we know, there had been a steady amount of trade on the river over the previous centuries, every village along the banks having its own wharf and relying on the hoys or other craft for supplies of every kind and for transporting its products. However, with the establishment of the Canal Company in 1742 and the possibility of goods travelling right to and from Tonbridge, there was an even greater interest in the use of canals and rivers. There was also understandable realisation that to cut across from the Medway direct to the Thames by canal would save miles and miles of transit, all the way down to Sheerness and round the Isle of Grain — the Nore. Plans were drawn up and in the year of Trafalgar (1805) a start was made on the eight mile stretch, for that is all it was, but it was not long before the difficulty of cutting a tunnel through the chalk hills around Higham had to be faced. It was this tunnel, 3,931 yards in length, that held up the work for so long and made the whole project rather costly. However in 1824 the Thames and Medway Canal was opened to traffic and the first barges passed through. With the amount of paper, cement and other materials being sent through to the great London market, to say nothing of the fish and agricultural produce, one would have thought that this canal would have been extensively used, but that was not so at all. Possibly the difficulty of "tracking" a barge through the tunnel by hand, towing behind a horse or, later, using a steam tug was the limiting factor. In any case the last named would have filled it with fumes for only the most simple ventilation shafts were used and a tunnel over two miles in length speedily becomes sulphurous. A further problem was that the use of a steam tug tended to erode the tow-path and damage the brick-work. Unfortunately, then, this project proved a failure and after only eighteen years the Thames and Medway Canal Company investigated the possibility of using the tunnel as a railway track. At first only a single line was laid, using half the width of the tunnel, but finally the whole was filled in to form a double track line between Stroud and Gravesend and then on to Dartford, Erith and London.

Just the other side of Higham village from the tunnel is Gad's Hill Place, the house immortalised by Charles Dickens, and this seems the right moment to mention something about his association with Rochester before we leave Bridge Reach. Very many books have been written about the life of the great novelist, the Dickens Fellowship both in Rochester and in Broadstairs holds many meetings, readings from his works and arranges performances of *Oliver Twist* and other favourites on the stage. A Dickens' Week is an annual commemoration of his life and times when members of the Broadstairs society parade in period costumes, and suitable events take place.

Higham Canal basin. The canal tunnel, now a railway tunnel, can be seen in the background.
Clive Lawford

Dickens was devoted to Rochester, as he was also to the Kent coast and he had a genuine love and understanding of the sea, doubtless derived from his earliest years when his father was appointed to Chatham dockyard and when he accompanied him in the navy pay-yacht on a trip to Sheerness. From 1836 until 1851 he made frequent trips down to Broadstairs, for the first few years travelling by steamer from London Bridge Wharf. It appears from his instructions to his friend John Foster, who was planning to visit him there, that the steamer would heave to off Broadstairs if requested and a boatman in a wherry would put off and take passengers ashore.

By the time he was thinking of purchasing Gad's Hill Place, however, the railways had very largely cut out the steamer service and the old-established stage coaches as well, and he was able to travel from London direct to Higham station which was quite near the house. Ever since he had passed it as a boy when travelling from Chatham with his father, he had felt an admiration for it, a certainty that one day, if only he worked hard enough, he would either own that house or one very like it. Sometimes when he seized a week-end down at Rochester, probably staying at the old coaching inn named the *Bull* which was re-named the *Royal Victoria and Bull Hotel* after the Queen had stayed there in 1838, made famous in the *Pickwick Papers*, he would tramp up to Gad's Hill to see if by chance the house was empty. He was an inveterate walker and when friends came down with him for a week-end he would tramp them rapidly about, exploring the old castle, the Cathedral and all the fortifications on the one day and then heading up above Strood to Gad's Hill and on to Cobham Park the next. Perhaps also he might vary things with a walk up the eastern bank of the river, cutting across Bluebell Hill and past Kit's Coty House to Maidstone, seven miles of the most beautiful scenery in England, he thought.

When, finally the chance came and he saw an opportunity of fulfilling his life's ambition, he wrote to John Foster in 1856, "I was better pleased with Gadshill Place last Saturday on going down there even than I had prepared myself to be." One can sense in the letter his excitement at the prospect that the house might soon be his as he adds about the surrounding country, "there is no healthier (marshes avoided) and in my eyes more beautiful. One of these days I shall show you some places up the Medway with which you will be charmed."

Once the house was safely his, he made numerous improvements. It had been built originally by a certain Mr Stevens in 1780, an ostler who had come up in the world by marrying the widow of the inn-keeper by whom he was employed, and then turning to brewing. The Rochester area has always been a centre of brewing among other trades with a number of small firms being gradually overshadowed by such larger concerns as Mr Style's Medway Brewery or Mr Winch of Best's Brewery, Chatham. This man Stevens did so well that he became, as he put it, "Mare" of Rochester. The idea in the back of Dickens' mind was to improve the property and then re-let it but he speedily grew so attached to it that he decided to make it his permanent home. He built on a drawing room and dug a tunnel under the road to lead through to a shrubbery where, in a Swiss chalet-type structure, he used to write surrounded by the trees and all the sounds of the countryside. As it was a fairly lonely spot he had a succession of guard dogs, never less than two and sometimes even more. There is a delightful description of a particular couple of Newfoundlands when he took them down to the river, in a letter quoted by John Foster. "When they get into the Medway," he writes, "it is hard to get them out again. The other day Bumble (the son) got into difficulties among some floating timber and became frightened. Don (the father) was standing by me, shaking off the wet and looking on carelessly, when all of a sudden he perceived something amiss, and went in with a bound and brought Bumble out by the ear. The scientific way in which he towed him along was charming."

A final memory of Charles Dickens is amusing. He very soon became a general favourite with all the local inhabitants round Gad's Hill Place and when his younger daughter was to be married, they all turned out in force. The carriages could scarcely get to and from the little church because of the triumphal arches under which they had to pass, John Foster tells us. However the culmination of the whole episode occurred after the service, when Dickens was on his way back to the house. The blacksmith had managed to acquire a couple of small cannon which he had concealed in his forge and at the appropriate moment he loosed them off. "I doubt," says Foster, "if the shyest of men was ever so taken aback at an ovation."

During the span of his life, Charles Dickens had seen the transport of goods in the Medway area alter considerably, the rail taking the place of the stage coach, steam taking the place of sail; but above all there had been an extraordinary increase in manufacture of every kind. Early in the 1800s, there was really very little in Rochester—apart from the work connected with the dockyard at Chatham just downstream; but by the 1870s there were cattle-cake makers, soap manufacturers, mineral water works, carriage and bicycle makers and even a considerable clothing factory in addition to all the cement works, paper makers, and engineering concerns referred to already. Barge and boat-building was still carried on in the Rochester neighbourhood—just as Chatham only such a short way downstream was closely involved with the naval dockyard.

We have already referred to the way in which the big cement makers frequently had their own fleets of spritsail barges, sound sturdy vessels, well built and well maintained. Another industry which utilised similar barges was the brick-making trade, and here, too, the companies frequently had their own shipwrights and building yards. Quite a number of barges were built up at Maidstone but very many more at Rochester and along the Lower Medway.

Now, although the cargoes for which these barges were used have been diverted to other speedier methods of conveyance, there is a great upsurge of interest in the sprits'l barge, and a fair number have been rescued and reorganised as charter craft. Others have been converted to roomy barge-yachts, enthusiasts have opened up the Dolphin Yard as a museum on Milton Creek, the Thames Barge Sailing Club and the Society for Spritsail Barge Research have rapidly increasing membership. What is the peculiar allure which makes so many people's interest turn to what, after all, was a working-boat, frequently carrying grimy muddy cargoes or stacks of hay? Possibly it has to do with the amazing sailing properties of these very simple vessels, perhaps also their picturesque appearance for to see a barge creaming along with her ochre mains'l swelling in the wind, fores'l drawing well and a ruffle of foam at the bows is a thrilling sight. There is, however, another feature which appeals especially in these days of thin sheet-metal and glass reinforced plastic, their amazing solidity and the fascination of hand-worked timbers. Famous builders like John Curel of Frindsbury, Edmund Watson of Acorn Wharf and R. Horsnaill of Strood, all of them established round about

Sailing barges *Maid of Connaught* (left) and *Arrow*. *Alan Cordell*

the time of Trafalgar or Waterloo, set to work with the most simple equipment and frequently just on a hard bank which sloped down to the water. There would be a sawpit where the timbers would be cut, and stem and stern posts, spars and masts would be shaped with an adze, otherwise the only equipment would be a boiler to generate stream and soften the planks so that they could be shaped to the bows. There was no question of plans or drawings; the shipwrights were so skilled that they could provide a craft to order simply by eye — and she would be within a matter of inches of the dimensions required. Of course like all sailing-boats each one had its own peculiar qualities, some would beat up better to windward than others, others would be "wet" or dirty and throw up water over the bows, but all of them would be works of art in their own particular way and of massive strength. If properly cared for and maintained the life of such a barge would be a good fifty to sixty years — and there are several afloat now well over that age.

What really gave a spurt to barge-building was the increasing demand for cement and bricks for the rapidly increasing building projects in London. Here, in Kent, apart from the extensive cement interests already mentioned, we had the advantage of many good seams of brick earth. An example of the expansion of this trade is to be found in the firm of Eastwoods which started in quite a small way as ballast and builders merchants on the South Bank of the Thames, where the Festival Hall is now, in about 1815. Steadily they expanded, taking in brick-fields at Frindsbury, Conyer, Teynham and Lower Halstow at the latter place establishing a barge-building yard. Gradually, too, their fleet of barges increased so that by the turn of the century they could supply hundreds of thousands of bricks to almost any site up and down the Thames, Medway or the creeks of Kent and Essex, working far up the little runnels and inlets on the tide, resting up against some little wharf or hard and off-loading their cargo very close to where the bricks were needed. Bricks for the construction of the Wembley Stadium were worked round by barge from Rainham, thousands of Conyer bricks were used in buildings in London, such as the House of Commons, and vast numbers went into housing schemes, warehouses, factory chimneys and the like. Most of these were the well-known Kentish stock brick which hardened up well in the London air and were used extensively.

Among the barge-builders there grew up a strong family tradition, just as there did among the astonishingly skilful barge skippers who, with just a mate and a boy, or latterly with only a mate, would work their 80 foot long craft up the narrowest creeks or inlets. Then, laden with a return cargo, they could head out into the open, threshing their way through the lumpy seas of the Thames Estuary and working their tides up the Medway to Rochester or beyond. Local sailing lore of every kind was handed on from skipper to mate, tricks of current and tide that could only be discovered through long experience. The River

Medway had many peculiarities, which sometimes led to unexpected variations of course, particularly above Rochester Bridge where "land water"—a flush of rain draining down-stream—was a well known problem giving a flowing tide in the upper layer while the bottom layer was still running down. More interesting still was a "tide-gauge" known to the barge skippers which was explained to me in detail by Pat O'Driscoll, then a bargeman and now Editor of *Coast and Country*. Beneath the piers of Rochester Bridge are copings under which come courses of flag-stones. To allow sufficient tide to help them up as far as New Hythe and give them time to swing at the dolphin (marker post) and take up their berth by the gantries, the skippers would get under way when four courses of stones were showing on the flood tide. My informant once just scraped up in the *Olive May* when only two courses were showing, but that was cutting it very fine! Sadly some barges ended their days on the iron-hard sands of the Estuary, among them the *Vera* which went onto the West Barrow in 1952 as was recounted in *The Sound of Maroons*. She was built at Limehouse in 1898, but was Rochester owned, by the old London and Rochester Trading Company, a firm which from its start as Gill & Sons in 1858 was barge building and barge owning until as Crescent Shipping it has extended its cargo handling right up the east coast of England to all the smaller harbours and even across to the Rhine and the Maas.

The barges known as "brickies" which went up the London river with bricks would usually bring back a return load of the repulsive material known as "rough stuff", coke, ashes and household refuse of all sorts which, when

One of the popular paddle steamers on the Medway, the *City of Rochester*, sunk by an enemy mine dropped from an aircraft on 19th May, 1941. *E. D. G. Payne*

piled ashore at the brickfields, would heat up and cause an appalling smell; but it was a very excellent fuel for the brick-kilns and, as F. W. Willmott mentions in his *Bricks and Brickies*, the local lads were able to earn a few pence sorting out old glass and bits of china useless for burning. There is a "glass bottle beach" at Halstow where such hard core was thrown.

Several of the Rochester and Strood barge yards also built the local dobles and bawleys which went out shrimping and smelt-fishing, and of course there were also numerous sail-makers who supplied the ochred canvas for the barges. Among the larger builders in the heyday of the barges were Messrs G. Gill and Sons, of Acorn Wharf (just mentioned) who, with the launch of *Dinah* in 1894, had passed the fifty mark. In addition, many of the cement works and the brickmakers were building their own, several companies having as many as sixty or seventy in their fleet.

As the building industry slackened after the First World War and we ran into the years of depression the barge building industry also suffered; but even in the Second World War a number of these craft were pressed into use as mooring-vessels for barrage balloons and as such did splendid service. The *Kingfisher* was one of these—she was badly damaged when a German aircraft was shot down and crashed into her, demolishing her stern. She was towed off to Stansgate Creek and beached where her remains still lie. Others were used as lighters or for powder storage. After the war those that were left were often in need of re-rigging or repair and there was very little trade for them; so

The steam coaster *Robin* of 366 tons, built at Blackwall in 1890, is shown here at Doust's yard, Rochester, in 1976 when restoration work was three-quarters finished. This work has since been completed for the Maritime Trust, which has her on display with other historic ships in the St Katherine's Dock, London. *Maritime Trust*

either they were cut down to motor-barges, converted to house-boats or hulked in lonely creeks. Some even ended up as part of a re-built sea-wall. But even when lying disconsolate in some muddy bed, the strength of the timbers, the sturdy rudders and massive stems have a strange fascination.

Not only barges were built by Messrs Gill for in 1898 the Medway Yacht Club accepted a challenge from an Australian yacht owner, with his *Irex*. The well-known marine artist W. L. Wyllie, who was at that time Commodore, commissioned Gill's to build a specially designed yacht to meet this challenge and in due course the *Maid of Kent* was launched. She was altogether revolutionary in design and an entire contrast to the heavily built Australian *Irex*, being referred to by Mrs Wyllie as a "skimming dish". There was a great deal of interest and enthusiasm among yachtsmen over this challenge and on the days fixed for the races large crowds assembled to watch, but the *Maid of Kent* proved infinitely superior to the other craft, winning every race.

It would be quite impossible to mention all the many builders and repairers who have worked, or in many cases, are still working in Rochester; firms like the London and Rochester Trading Company already mentioned still build tugs and barges and also handle repair work as well as managing large coastwise fleets. Acorn Wharf is still busy and there are also shipbreaking interests on the river. The *Athina B* which ran onto the beach at Brighton during a storm in the winter of 1979-80, the crew being rescued with the utmost difficulty by the Shoreham Harbour lifeboat in a service which earned Coxswain Ken Voice the silver medal, was finally towed to the Medway for breaking up having provided the restaurant and café owners of Brighton with an unexpected winter bonus. The spectacle of this quite large vessel of 1,100 tons high and dry on the shore aroused intense interest, attracting visitors from far and wide. Another ship which was at Rochester for a thorough overhaul and reconditioning was the old coaster *Robin* which was purchased a few years ago by the Maritime Trust from her Spanish owners with the idea of preserving

The paddle steamer *Medway Queen* in River Medina, Isle of Wight. *E. D. G. Payne*

her at St Katherine's Dock as an example of the steam coaster of the late nineteenth century. She was originally built at Blackwall in 1890 for British owners, of gross registered tonnage of 366, powered by triple expansion reciprocating engines. After reconditioning and being restored to her original appearance she was taken round to St Katherine's Dock under her own power. There she will certainly be a great attraction as the oldest British steam coaster in full working order.

Yet another famous vessel that used to lie off the Esplanade is the spritsail barge *Cambria*, which has now sailed round to St Katherine's also. She was originally built at Greenhithe in 1906 by William Everard while his brother Fred worked on her twin the *Hibernia*. The latter finished up stranded on the Norfolk coast in a howling gale; but *Cambria* carried on trading for Everards until 1954 when Captain Bob Roberts took her over, running her till 1971 when he passed her over to the Maritime Trust. It is inspiring to know that this handsome little barge is in the Trust's safe keeping for she was the last purely sailing vessel to carry cargoes, many of them in and out of the Port of Rochester.

There was one final feature of Rochester round about the turn of the century that should not be forgotten and of which there is a reminder in yet another shipbuilding and repairing firm, the New Medway Company, formerly owning paddle steamers. For years just below the railway bridge one used to see their *Medway Queen* moored, a reminder of the paddle steamer services that were a regular feature of Rochester as well as of many south east coastal resorts. Frequently referred to as the Medway packet she or one of her sisters would make regular sailings down to Sheerness and across the estuary to Southend. The years before the First World War were the great days of the paddlers, when *Audrey* beat her way down the estuary to Sheerness, the General Steam Navigation Company operated their route from London round to Margate and Ramsgate, and the Belle steamers plied across the Thames Estuary visiting Southend, Herne Bay and Margate on Thursdays and Sheerness and Rochester on Fridays. The paddlers with their white churning wake were quite a thrilling spectacle, very sturdy sea-boats and not at all inclined to roll because of the width across at the paddle-boxes, although they could certainly pitch. *Medway Queen* herself was taken down to the river Medina in the Isle of Wight and though some repair work has been done to her she is still not in a seaworthy condition. It would be a pleasant link with past history, however, if that particular vessel could be brought back to the Medway for, with the white horse of Kent prancing on her buff funnel, she went across to Dunkirk in the early days of June 1940 and took more than seven thousand of our troops off the beaches in that most memorable evacuation. She deserves to be restored to her home port of Rochester or perhaps to the care of the Martime Trust.

CHAPTER ELEVEN

Dockyard and Defences

MENTION of Chatham immediately brings to mind the Royal Navy, and the famous dockyard,* the *Victory* and other great ships of Nelson's day. Whereas the story of Rochester is traced far back into history, the same cannot really be said of its sister-town. Principally of course this has to do with Rochester's position at the traditional crossing of the river, on the line of the Roman road between Dover (and Richborough), London and the North, defended successively by Roman and medieval walls, the crucial bridge commanded by the massive keep of the Norman castle. There is, too, and no less important, the ancient founding of the Cathedral at a time when bishops wielded mighty power spiritually, and frequently temporally as well, the Priory close by the Cathedral, the ecclesiastical importance of the place as the second See in the county. Chatham had none of these but with Gillingham next door had the inestimable advantage of a wide sweep of river without any hampering bridge or shallow ford, a completely rock-free river bed of good firm mud and surrounding groups of hills which provided plenty of shelter from stormy south-westerly winds. Thus as soon as any concerted attempt was made to establish regular warships, as opposed to the armed merchant-vessels hurriedly pressed into service by the Cinque Ports in time of war, this anchorage presented considerable advantages as a base, especially when potential enemies were in the region of the Low Countries. Here it would be safe for warships to lie at anchor, in good holding-ground, within easy distance of London. Here, too, they could ride in-shore on the tide and, when it ebbed, repairs or maintenance work could be done on their timbers. Neighbouring Gillingham and Rainham have plenty of early associations, especially with the Jutish settlers, Rainham having a Saxon church founded in 871, and the present church with many Early English features has the unusual dedication to St Margaret of Antioch. Gillingham's earliest church also went back to the Saxon times and the present parish church is largely of fifteenth century date. Here also was a special building devoted to the needs of the archbishops when they were travelling the land, known as the Archibishop's Palace.

We can see, then, Saxon and Norman settlements hereabouts, and a small riverside community governed by the Lord of the Manor with judicial authority vested in a High Constable, a certain Ralf Fitz Thorold being the first to hold office in 1070. Apart from general references to men of

*In line with Government defence cuts the present suggestion is that this great naval establishment should be run down.

Gillingham taking part in Wat Tyler's rebellion in 1381 and also in Jack Cade's rising in 1450, history for this group of towns begins with the Tudor navy.

Whether or not the *Henri Grâce à Dieu*, the *Great Harry* as she is more generally known, was built in this neighbourhood is uncertain. Her building date is supposedly 1488. She was a two-decker with three masts and was reputed to be the first warship, as such, constructed in England, being the backbone of the Royal Navy started under Henry VII and further developed under Henry VIII. The first definite mention of any naval establishment here is a reference to the hiring of storehouses at "Jillingham" in 1547, and ships were to be removed from Portsmouth to "Jillingham Water" to be grounded and caulked a few years later. At that time there was no recognised anchorage for the fleet—but vessels were moored up off Deptford, Woolwich, Greenwich and elsewhere on the Thames and also at Portsmouth, though this last named place was inconvenient owing to the distance from London.

It was not until the reign of Queen Elizabeth I that "Jillingham" or Chatham was selected as one of the most suitable centres and steps were taken to rent and purchase land for stores. Elizabeth ascended the throne at a most critical time for England when we had just lost our last outpost on the European mainland, Calais, when religious antagonisms had set every man against his fellow, when the exchequer was bankrupt. Yet out of all this, by diplomatic skill and courage, she managed to restore confidence and a living sense of adventure and daring while at the same time avoiding the extravagance of war even though we were threatened with hostility on every side. Very early on in her reign she gave instructions for a castle to be built at Upnor, just a

Upnor Castle. *Clive Lawford*

H.M.S. *Victory*, built at Chatham in 1765, afloat in Portsmouth Harbour at the beginning of the twentieth century. *National Maritime Museum*

little way downstream from Chatham to guard the ships lying at anchor or re-fitting. Richard Watts of Rochester was given the supervision of the work and by about 1571 the castle, three storeys high, crenellated and with round towers at the four corners was in being. There were guard rooms, stores and embrasures for cannon while a great chain was prepared to be slung across to a massive hook on the opposite bank to catch the keel of any unwary attacker.

The castle is still there, having been used as a powder-store in later years, greystone among the green trees, a strange reminder of these far off days while yachts glide on the Medway in front of it and until fairly recently the four towering masts of the training ship *Arethusa** soared sky-ward. Painted black with a white band and what looked like gun ports she was a splendid training-centre run by the Shaftesbury Homes for young seamen who went scampering up and down the ratlines, lay out along the great yards and very soon acquired a foretaste of what life at sea meant. Incongruously she was really a "Cape Horner", not a warship at all. Originally built by Blohm and Voss in 1911 she was christened *Peking* and sailed with the *Pamir, Parma* and *Passat* on the world-wide cargo routes of the famous German Laeisz line. Though never captained by the legendary Hilgendorf her last skipper had

*The Royal Navy's fourth ship to bear the name *Arethusa* was built at Pembroke in 1849, 4th rate of 50 guns. After naval service she was loaned to Baroness Burdett-Coutts in 1873 as a training ship for destitute boys. Later she was managed by the Shaftesbury Homes until 1932 and broken up in 1933 by Mr Copley Hewett's men, as we have seen in Chapter Seven. Her replacement, the *Peking*, was re-named *Arethusa*.

been trained by him; but then in 1932 with sail rapidly giving way to steam she was purchased as a training-ship and her noble silhouette was a spectacular sight off Upnor till she was sold to American interests in 1975.

While yet the Chatham base was in its infancy, there arrived on the Medway a family from Tavistock which had had to leave their house Crowndale Farm because of religious persecution. The father became vicar of the little out-of-way village of Upchurch down beyond Horsham marsh, his son Francis went to sea in a small cargo hoy plying from Rochester along the coasts and even across to foreign ports. So Francis Drake instead of "sailing the Devon seas" as is said in the famous poem by Sir Henry Newbolt actually learnt his seamanship in the tidal estuary of the Medway and among the tumbling white-horses of the English Channel. It is appropriate that one of our greatest

The sailing barge *Cambria* (109 tons), built by Everards' at Greenhithe in 1906. The last barge to trade regularly under sail, she was purchased by the Maritime Trust in 1971 and is now in St Katherine's Dock. She is seen here at Lower Upnor with the *Arethusa* (ex *Peking*) in the background. *Fine Art Studio*

sailors should have had his first taste of sail so close to the great naval yard of Chatham, and we remember that other great sailor Nelson who also went aboard his first ship in these same waters. Drake learnt his trade fast and on the death of the skipper and owner of the little cargo-vessel was amazed to find that it had been bequeathed to him by his late employer.

With the threat of war with Spain looming ever closer Queen Elizabeth I herself came down to inspect the progress of works on two occasions and she also set up a Commission including such far-sighted and experienced men as Burghley, Walsingham, and Lord Howard as well as the practical and daring sea-captains Drake and Martin Frobisher to hurry on the work at Chatham so that a whole squadron could be supplied and fitted out there with the minimum of delay. It was also decided to start building here and by a few years before the Armada there is a record of a pinnace being launched, the *Sunne* of 59 tons. This was the start of a great tradition of naval building which meant employment for considerable numbers of people in the area and which gradually led to the extension of the dockyard with every associated trade of smithy, rope and sail-making all included in the same compound. This Elizabethan yard was situated directly in front of St Mary's church and is now more or less entirely absorbed by office buildings and the Public Library. The old Gunwharf which stretched from a point nearly opposite Chatham Town Hall for about a quarter of a mile was sold in 1959 to private industry but beyond that the dockyard proper extends right into Gillingham, covering some five hundred acres including the Great Basins and St Mary's Island. However at the start of our survey it was still very small and not until James I's time was any sort of a dock involved, a wet dock to take four galleys being formed by dredging and closing off one of the creeks. Now came the leasing of a further seventy acres of land, a dry-dock, store-houses, a sail-loft and workshops being established. Gradually more and more land was taken in, a rope-walk was formed, at first outside the other stores, but later it became a rope-house. Great stores of timber were gathered here, coming down by water, and were there stacked to season. The tale of ships built began to grow. After a spell of stagnation in the early part of the seventeenth century, Phineas Pett (1570-1647) built the enormous three decked *Sovereign of the Seas* round at Deptford which served for the next sixty years in the Royal Navy, frequently coming into Chatham for re-fitting, and where Phineas was assistant master shipwright in 1603, and Peter Pett (1610-1672), his son, became Commissioner of the Navy at Chatham being frequently visited by the King and by Samuel Pepys. Another son, Christopher, (1620-68) was master shipwright at Woolwich and Deptford whilst a grandson, Phineas (1628-78), became master shipwright at Chatham.

During the Commonwealth with a great increase in sea power under Admiral Blake the yard was busy, and shortly after the Restoration Charles II was here to inspect his new 100 gun *Royal Sovereign*. However stringent economies caused many of the warships to be laid up in the Medway just at the time when an attack from Holland appeared imminent.

Then there occurred the most humiliating action in our history when the Dutch Admiral De Ruyter appeared off the Gunfleet in the Thames Estuary with sixty sail on 7th April 1667. In face of this threat the King commanded the Duke of Albermarle, who, as General Monk had been chiefly instrumental in bringing about the Restoration, to take supreme command to defend London, and the ships in the Medway. There was some little delay before the Dutch actually advanced on Sheerness while they were making tentative explorations into the Thames but all the ships there had been withdrawn well up-river, and if the state of the defences had not been so chaotic perhaps a better defence would have been offered. However, as it was, Vice Admiral Spragge at Sheerness only put up a token resistence. For a matter of one and half hours the Dutch ships bombarded the place, there being only about seven guns in the English fort that could be used, and some of these apparently jumped their mountings with the recoil., Then when he learned that eight hundred men had been landed under a renegade, Admiral Spragge withdrew leaving the enemy to plunder the place. They seized stores and provisions and broke down the sea-walls so that the whole area was flooded, before moving on up the river to Chatham.

Meanwhile frantic efforts had been made to block the passage of the enemy by a chain in Gillingham Reach, by sinking block ships and by arranging for the chain at Upnor Castle to be guarded by the naval vessel *Unity*. Just above this chain were more first-raters but a number of warships were towed higher up the river. The main reasons for such ineffective defence was that the major part of our fleet was out of commission owing to the cut in defence spending. So it was that once the Dutch had burst through the Gillingham chain and overwhelmed the *Matthias* and *Charles V* on guard there, they manoevred more or less uninterruptedly among the block ships, finding a way through. To avoid their falling into enemy hands, the *Loyal London, Royal James* and *Royal Oak* had been sunk at their moorings. Now the Dutch inflicted the final humiliation in seizing the *Royal Charles*, the fine 82 gunner that had brought the King back from exile, and she was taken away as a prize. In the face of increasing artillery fire from land and fearing that his luck would turn, De Ruyter made off as soon as the tide served. This miserable experience roused people to the danger and within a month rigorous efforts were being made to re-fortify Sheerness. A great spurt of acitivity began at Chatham, the dockyard being extended still further and the King himself and Prince Rupert visited to inspect the work. During all this time Hill House, which was situated fronting the present Dock Road, was the Admiralty House providing offices for the naval authorities, lodging for senior officers and also for such important visitors as Samuel Pepys, who refers to it frequently in his diary. It continued to be used in this way for at least one hundred and fifty years until finally demolished to make way for the Royal Marines barracks.

By the early eighteenth century the dockyard had become our main naval base and the stores, rope-walks, mast-ponds for keeping spars, forges for anchors and chains, appeared to Daniel Defore "like a well-ordered city". But it was the Seven Years' War and later the Napoleonic Wars that gave such a great impetus to the work of the dockyard. And along with the improved facilities there, the number of people employed increased, houses spread in all directions, the village of Brompton extended in size till it joined up with Chatham and Royal Marine and Royal Engineers barracks were built. However there were also serious silting problems in the river, so the emphasis seems to have been on building rather than general repair work for a time. It is interesting to note some of the famous ships built here: *The Prince*, one of Phineas Pett's great ships, *The Royal George*, Admiral Hawkes' flagship at Quiberon, the *Formidable*, flagship of Admiral Rodney, and greatest of all of course H.M.S. *Victory*. "Heart of oak are our ships" as the old song says, and *Victory* which took six years to build is supposed to have involved seven hundred oaks, which had been lying seasoning in the yard. Launched on the

Launch of H.M.S. *Waterloo* at Chatham. *Chatham Public Library*

7th of May 1765 this magnificent vessel was thus forty years old at the time of her most famous action at Trafalgar and was at that time considered the pride of the fleet. Further mention must be made here of Lord Nelson for it is so approrpirate that he should have joined his first ship at the very place where *Victory* was born.

When his uncle Captain Maurice Suckling was written to* with a suggestion of sea-faring experience for the boy, he replied, "What has poor Horace done, who is so weak, that he above all the rest should be sent to rough it out at sea? But let him come . . ." This far from enthusiastic welcome was the prelude to a most inauspicious start to Horatio's naval career. In early spring 1771 he went up to London with his father, was put onto the Chatham coach and duly set down there with the rest of the passengers. He, aged twelve, then set off for the water-side realising that he would have to find his way aboard somehow. Having in the end located the 64 gun *Raisonnable*, lying at moorings just a short way off the building slip where *Victory* had been launched some six years before, he was wandering about somewhat at a loss as to how to get aboard when an officer noticed him, saw how chilled and disconsolate he looked, and took him home to give him some refreshments. With this help he was soon able to go aboard, but Captain Suckling was not in the ship, was not expected for several days and nobody had been told about Horatio's arrival. As Southey says, "He paced the deck for the remainder of the day without being noticed by anyone . . ."

In spite of such a poor start, Horatio soon came to know the waters of the Medway intimately and it is very likely that his understanding and appreciation of soundings, that sixth sense he possessed about where a ship could or could not be floated and which was so invaluable to him at the Battle of Copenhagen, was acquired in his very early years' experience in our river. For ten years as a Thames pilot he was in and out of the Medway, the Nore, Sheerness, down to the North Foreland, always on the move. By 1781 he had the *Albemarle* as his first command and was being transferred to the off-shore anchorage in the Downs off Deal that he was to come to know so well. It was to these same waters that *Victory* bore him home after his death in action off Cape Trafalgar, and off the Nore that his body was trans-shipped to the *Chatham* for carriage up the Thames to its final resting place. After lying for some while at moorings in Portsmouth harbour, *Victory* was finally saved from further deterioration and placed in the dry dock where she now stands for all to see thanks to the enthusiasm of the "Save the Victory" campaign started by Admiral of the Fleet Sir Doveton Sturdee. Further, due to the enthusiasm and skill of the technical committee under Sir Philip Watts, she was restored very much to her original state.

Another very famous vessel from the Chatham area, Frindsbury in this case, was H.M.S. *Bellerophon*, a 74 gun ship designed by Sir Thomas Slade

**Life of Nelson,* Robert Southey.

who had also designed the *Victory*, launched on 8th October 1786, which was soon involved in action during the Napoleonic Wars. She was in The Glorious First of June (1794), that great engagement in which Lord Howe seized six French vessels and sank another. Her next major engagement was in the Mediterranean where she was one of Nelson's squadron that pursued Napoleon's fleet to Aboukir Bay, and she was hotly engaged with the flagship *L'Orient* shortly before that vessel blew up. Again she was at Trafalgar, in the line of ships led by Admiral Collingwood, and after being in the thick of the battle and taking two prizes she was given the honour of escorting *Victory* back to England. However the event which is chiefly conncected with her occurred ten years later when, on 15th July 1815 she was lying in Basque Roads, part of the estuary of the French river Charente, under Captain Maitland and a shore boat came alongside with the Emperor Napoleon in the stern sheets. Formally he surrendered his sword to Captain Maitland on the quarter deck, a dramatic moment at the conclusion of years of warfare. It is sad to think that only a few months later, in October, this fine ship was a prison hulk laden with prisoners and convicts lying at Sheerness.

The rate of buildings during the Napoleonic Wars had been considerable, some fourteen ships being completed at Chatham dockyard. At the same time numerous private yards were also building for the Navy under contract. H.M.S. *Bellerophon* had been built by Greaves and Nicholson at Frindsbury, they had also launched H.M.S. *Meleager* the year before. The same Nicholson had a smaller yard where he built three other small ships. Another builder John Pelham had a yard right next door to Greaves and he launched eight warships between 1807 and 1815, the largest being H.M.S. *Romney* of 58 guns. Several other private yards in the Frindsbury—Chatham Ness area were also hard at work, and at Upnor John King launched as many as sixteen in six years including two 74 gun ships. Another well-known builder was Charles Ross at Acorn Wharf, who had previously built several merchant vessels, including some for the Hudson's Bay Company. He built two 38 gun frigates, but after his death his wife carried on the yard, building H.M.S. *Vigo* and H.M.S. *Stirling Castle*, both of 74 guns together with several smaller vessels, bomb ships and the like. J. M. Preston in this *Industrial Medway* makes the point that whereas seventy warships were launched from private yards during the Napoleonic Wars, Chatham dockyard itself was only responsible for fourteen. But this is understandable in view of the constant maintenance and repair work going on all the time in connection with the fleet stationed at the Nore.

The next few years saw the draining and enclosure of a large stretch of marshland to increase the size of the dockyard. Wet docks and graving docks were constructed and the latest designs in battleships were undertakan, altogether forty-six sailing ships being built between 1815 and 1832. Then

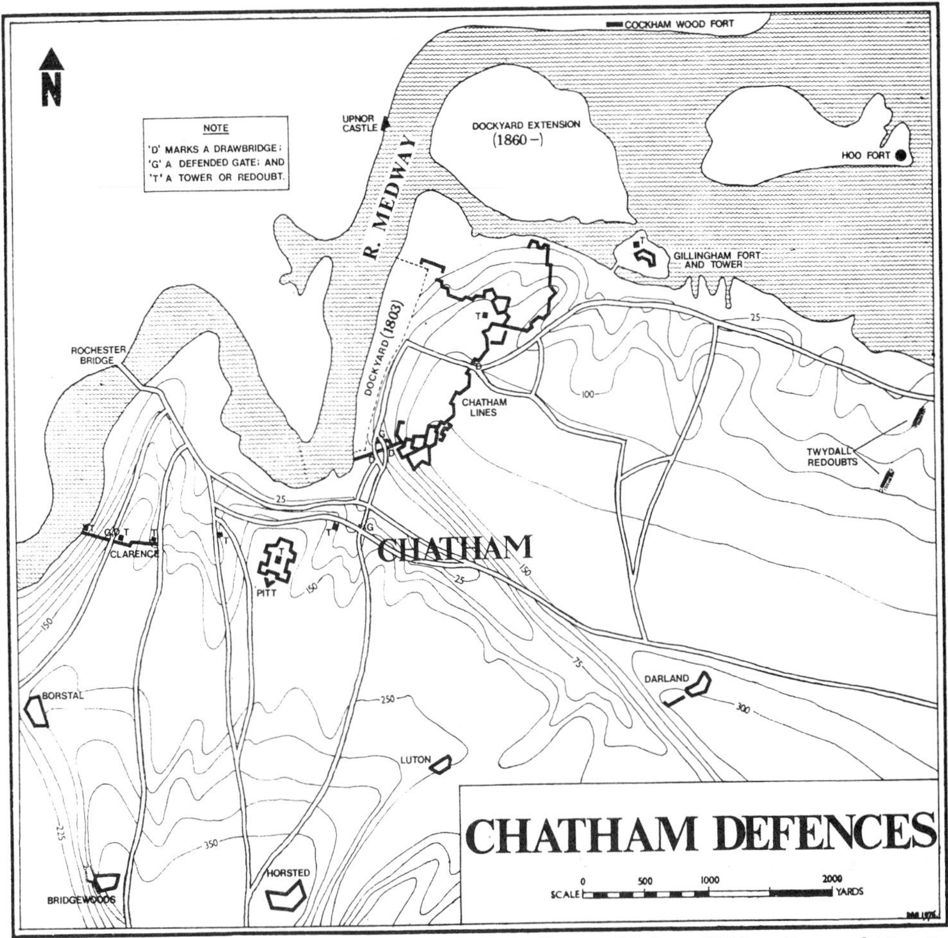

D. Barnes, Medway Military Research Group

came a change, for in 1833 the first steamer, the *Gleaner* of 351 tons was constructed, to be followed soon after by the paddle frigate H.M.S. *Tiger*. She was followed by the first iron battleship, H.M.S. *Achilles* of 6,000 tons, after which came specialised construction of submarines, and overhaul and refitting of such vessels is continued up to the present day. We can see therefore what an immense part Chatham has played in the development of the Navy and there is still very much of a naval presence there with modern repair facilities in among the older buildings which go back way beyond the Napoleonic Wars.

Because of the outstanding importance of this complex of building and re-fitting yards and basins, a thorough system of defensive lines was begun around the time of the Seven Years' War, this being extended and improved from time to time. There was no great likelihood of an attack being made up the Medway with strong fleets anchored off the Nore—and in any case Sheerness had been greatly strengthened to obviate trouble, but there was considerable anxiety about an attack being made from the landward side. Hence the great fortified entrenchments known as the Chatham Lines were constructed stretching along the hill above the dockyard for a mile, enclosing the village of Brompton, from the Medway shore in Gillingham Reach right across the neck of the dockyard peninsula to join the river again in Chatham Reach. At the northern end the hillslopes were defended by a two-fold system of trenchworks, the Lower and Inner bastions, with the Casemate Barracks in between. Then came the Great Lines, so called, and finally the Amherst Redoubt, Spur Battery and Cornwallis Battery. The three redoubts on the highest part of the ridge, which were sometimes called Fort Amherst, were so designed that they could be held in succession as some sort of a citadel. The ditches were twenty-seven feet wide with a nine foot parapet and were some eight feet deep, the whole construction being done by the Royal Engineers, and three gateways were made with bridges over the ditch. One of these led through to Chatham, one led to Gillingham by way of Brompton and the third was a sally port by which defenders could surge out to make surprise attacks on any besieging enemy. In addition to these redoubts and trenchworks special volunteer forces were formed known as the River and Sea Fencibles. As W. H. Lapthorne describes in an interesting article in *Coast and County*, these were the brain-child of Captain Horace Riggs Popham R.N. who put forward a

Copy of identity pass of Richard Payne, of the City of London River Fencibles, found during the demolition of an old cottage in Chatham. *W. H. Lapthorne*

No.41. A.D. 1812.

PRO REGE ET PATRIA — R F

RIVER FENCIBLES OF THE CITY OF LONDON.

MATTHIAS LUCAS, Esq. Commandant.

SOUTH DIVISION. FIRST COMPANY.

We hereby certify, That *Richard Payne*, C. 18.

Thirty eight Years of Age, *five* Feet, *seven* Inches high, *light* Complexion, *hazel* Eyes, *Lt brown* Hair, is a Member of this Corps, whose Offer of Service has been approved and accepted by His Majesty.

Matt^w Lucas

W Chapman Captain of Division.

W. Burgess Captain of Company.

Typical uniform of a member of the Cinque Ports Sea Fencibles. In the background are Fort cottages, near Bleak House, Broadstairs. Research into this little-known Corps was undertaken by local historian W. H. Lapthorne.
W. H. Lapthorne

plan for such a body in 1798. The King approved the formation of a Corps of Sea Fencibles its members being drawn from the longshoremen and inhabitants of coastwise towns, and the watermen of the Rivers then formed themselves into Corps of River Fencibles. An interesting sidelight on these volunteer forces was thrown by the discovery during the demolition of an old cottage in Chatham of an oilskin pouch containing the papers of one Richard Payne as a member of the City of London River Fencibles.

With further hostilities in the eighteenth century the Government made a thorough survey of the area and came to the conclusion that much additional defensive work should be done. All this was linked with the extra forts on the Thames Estuary, with the Royal Military Canal down at Hythe and the line of martello towers along the coast from Folkestone to Romney Marsh; and also the idea to use the Medway itself as a bastion of defence if necessary. The measures taken at Chatham were the strengthening of Fort Amherst and the digging of a great network of tunnels and magazines underneath the Cornwallis Battery, complete with entrances at various strategic points. The whole complex of Fort Amherst, its various faces covered by cross-fire from flanking galleries was an astonishing piece of military engineering, and later at great expense all ditches and ramparts were bricked.

Mercifully all these military preparations were not needed but during the Second World War the Civil Defence used the tunnels as their Medway

Headquarters, and considerable work was taking place in 1980 to try to restore at least Fort Amherst. Of a number of other fortifications built in the later nineteenth century not very much now remains. However they were all part of a defensive network to safeguard the city of Rochester, Chatham dockyard and the military headquarters. Fort Borstal, Fort Clarence, now largely destroyed but of which the tower is used for Post Office stores, Fort Pitt which is now the Medway Technical School for Girls, and the old blockhouse connected with it now no more and replaced by the Medway College of Design, all these were part of the ring of defence works. Fort Horsted is in fairly good condition still, Fort Luton has nearly gone, Fort Darland has all but vanished and now Fort Bridge woods is partially demolished. It is a pity when such memorials to the strenuous efforts of previous governments to keep England safe are allowed to wither and decay for they speak of a part of our heritage. Ugly arches and redoubts of brickwork as they are, they still have a certain historical value and to preserve Fort Amherst as an example of early nineteenth century military planning, with perhaps a detailed diagram of the whole system, would seem to be a worthy undertaking.

Now we have looped the river past Frindsbury, swung in the great curve past the Sun pier and surveyed the far-spreading Naval dockyard. All the way have been tiers of lighters, the ubiquitous coasters with engines aft, heavy diesels throbbing the evening air, tugs moored up waiting for orders to guide ships alongside wharves, all the business of a great mercantile river. How very different from the days when W. L. Wyllie and his wife were living at Hoo Lodge just the other side of the river from the dockyard, when they would embark in their small boat to slip across to the Admiral's stairs for entertainment or receptions in the dockyard, taking only about fifteen minutes under

H.M.S. *Achilles*, the first iron battleship to be built at Chatham. *National Maritime Museum*

Drawbridge of Fort Bridgewoods, which has now been demolished.
G. Harvey, Medway Military Research Group

oars. On the other hand to Royal Engineers balls and receptions or to those held by the Royal Marines it was a full seven miles by road, which in those days, 1887, meant a ride in a dog-cart or a lengthy trundle in the village wagonette with its two horses. Those who speed their dinghies with outboards would make nothing of the distance, and the modern car owner would think the life of a hundred years ago unbelievably slow. Yet does our speed, our frantic burning up of oil really improve life?

Now the estuary widens out, great banks of mud gleam, saltings and marsh are all about as the occasional lean grey shape of a frigate or guided missile destroyer slices the water. Great power stations loom on the northern shore, vast tankers stand out against the skyline moored up to the finger-like jetties which reach out from the land. There are clustering yacht moorings, surviving spritsail barges unfurl their ochred sails and ramp to and fro on the occasion of the Medway Race, yachtsmen who have worked in from the open sea or who have come across the Thames Estuary with a fair wind and are planning to cruise the upper reaches lower all gear ready for the cramped medieval bridges to come. Above all is the great wide arch of the sky, the distant view of Sheppey, the fascination of the creeks and banks and even in spite of sprawls of modern housing development the little villages with their forgotten quays.

CHAPTER TWELVE

Hoo to Medway Mouth

AT THE risk of going back on our tracks slightly we must take a look at the various Hoos and reflect on Samuel Ireland's comment* on the Hoo peninsula. "There is scarcely a gentleman's house, or even a clergyman living there, in consequence of the depth of the soil, the dirtiness of the roads and the unwholesome air rising from its neighbouring marshes". Why exactly the depth of soil should affect the dwellings of clergymen is not specified but certainly it is now a strange peninsula with all the mass of oil refineries and vast power stations on the Isle of Grain at the end of it. Mrs Wyllie in *We were One* referred to the delights of Hoo Lodge, the soft green of the fields and the beautiful air on their hill in 1886. Inhabitants of a very much earlier date were the Romans who, having fortified Rochester, would seem to have had some sort of an outpost camp over here to judge by a number of cremation burials and a considerable scatter of pottery. In Saxon and Norman times, too, Hoo St Werburgh must have been an important parish for it had responsibility for the upkeep of one of the piers of Rochester Bridge. Possibly some entirely different river level may have been the case in these early times as the marshes show distinct occupation strata and many more Samian ware fragments have been recovered along there. Now the waterside area speaks of great desolation, with islets, marshes, Hoo Fort, and little winding creeks, before we plunge into the world of industry, brickworks and power stations.

Who was this Saint Werburgh who gave her name to this rather bleak place? Daughter of King Wulfere of Mercia and Ermenilde, a Kentish princess, she was renowned for her piety and Christian beliefs at a time when the pagans were in the ascendency. One of these, a noble named Werbode, sought her hand in marriage and to strengthen his suit spun a false story to the King that his two sons were in league with Bishop Chad to overthrow him. The violent King Wulfere seized and slew the two young princes but then repented of his deed and tried to make amends by establishing Christian centres, the Abbey of Peterborough being one. Werburgh now entered a convent. The blackguard Werbode is understood to have reaped his due reward and died in misery. Ethelred, who succeeded Wulfere in 675, gave Werburgh charge over all religious foundations for women in his kingdom and it was then that she is supposed to have come to the Hoo peninsula to establish a convent here. There is a legend that she aided the farmers of Hoo who were losing their crops owing

*In his *Picturesque Views of the River Medway* 1830, quoted by Philip MacDougall in *Bygone Kent*.

to the depredations of geese. She spoke to the birds and they forthwith went away; so statues to the Saint are always shown with a goose. In the year 699 she died and her body was supposed to have been buried at Hoo.

All this is legend, hidden in the mists of long ago, but something more modern and certain is the existence of salt-panning in the Medway between Elizabeth I's time and the 1700s. There were two sites on the Isle of Grain and other ancient workings on the Isle of Sheppey too. This was an effort to produce sea-salt to remove our dependence on imported salt from France and Spain, most important at a time when we were frequently either in a state of near or actual war with these countries. Before the days of deep-freeze the salt was essential for preserving such items as meat and fish. The Medway pans were suitable as they had plenty of briny shallow water and supplies of timber from the Weald, and later coal brought down from Newcastle by sea direct to heat the pans. This industry continued till the early 1700s when Cheshire rock salt effectively took over the trade, it being reckoned that one ton of fuel would produce one ton of Cheshire salt, whereas it would take six tons of fuel to produce the same result in salt-pans such as those on the Medway. Saltpan Reach commemorates this former industry. The other Hoos, All Hallows and St Mary's have no particular association. Casting our eyes southward to the

Skeletons of barges, Deadman's Island. *Bleak House Archives*

creeks and marshes of the other shore we pause a moment to mention that the Royal Society for the Protection of Birds owns Northward Hill, High Halstow where they and the Nature Conservancy maintain over 130 acres of woodland and scrub which contain one of the largest heronries in the country where some 140 birds nest and rear their young. In addition this is a splendid reserve for warblers and, in the spring, the woodland thrills to the song of the nightingale, while shelduck and mallard breed and so do long-eared owls. It is astonishing to have the peace of these woodlands only a few miles from Rochester in the one direction and all the clangour of the vast industries of the Isle of Grain on the other.

Over on the southern shore of the Medway the winding creeks and channels present a labyrinth of little waterways. In the days of Francis Drake these marshes were more extensive but the mud diggers of the nineteenth century removed much of the marsh clay for cement manufacture making extra runnels of water which the tides have since scoured out. Also, excessively high tides have breached some of the sea-walls, so that Burntwick, Slayhills, Barksore and other marshes are now partially flooded at every tide and the breach is increased by the outflowing water. Here when the tide is low and the gleaming mudbanks reflect the sunlight, little groups of men and women are to be seen stooping about in the bed of the stream, diving their arms down into the mud of the bottom. For this is the old traditional "gryping", or in other words searching the ditches or trenches of water to grab flounders which are always caught like this, by hand. Some people find these fish delicious fried in breadcrumbs. Down on the marshes in 1951, 1955 and 1956 a rather strange group of Romano-British jars came to light, each one containing the bones of a puppy together with charcoal. There were altogether seven of these and one inference is that they may have been to do with some ritual associated with crops. On the other hand Romano-British inhabitants here were chiefly connected with the making of pottery which seems to invalidate such a theory.

Cherry, pear and apple blossom fill the countryside away from the water's edge and down near the river come several brickworks, at Funton for example, where the brick-earth was formed into tiles by our Romano-British ancestors to judge from the many fragments discovered. Lower Halstow nearby has a quaint little church almost at the water's edge, which has much Roman brick and tile in its walls. A small wharf here goes back to Eastwoods' brickworks and it is quite right to see a Thames barge here among the moorings for small craft. What is not at all so right is to see the skeletal remains of many sturdy craft which worked their passages up and down the seaways for so many years. The gloomy hulks rotting amid the sedge and mud speak sadly of an age of solidity and strength when 'built-in obsolescence' was not contemplated. Otterham Quay, Lower Halstow, Stangate Creek, Deadman's Island, at all these places the massive timbers loom out of the mud, the ripples steal round and in between the ribs. Grim thoughts as well as grim sights haunt these places. For out in the river between here and Sheerness lay the prison hulks, some of them in Short Reach between Upnor and St Mary's Island, others in Long Reach where the jetty of Kingsnorth Power Station now juts out like a great finger into the stream. In an article written in 1975 W. H. Lapthorne mentions in *East Coast Digest* (now *Coast and Country*) the fact that out of sixty ex-R.N. ships that had been cut down and used as prison hulks, half were in the Medway. By the end of the Napoleonic Wars there were no fewer than seventy thousand French prisoners of war all of whom had to be incarcerated somewhere. As I mentioned in *The Sound of Maroons*, Margate caves were used among other places, but the prison hulks accounted for a good number, the smaller ships taking four hundred and fifty, the larger eight hundred. It is estimated that half the P.O.W.s were in the hulks by the end of the wars and, of course, as Lapthorne says, in such confined quarters the mortality rate from cholera, smallpox or typhoid was considerable. The names Prisoners' Bank and Deadman's Island are easily understandable, for many of those who succumbed were interred in such places. After the surviving Frenchmen had been repatriated, the hulks were used as convict prisons for a

Drawing of a typical prison hulk by T. Allum. *W. H. Lapthorne*

time and it would be to one of these that Charles Dickens was referring when he wrote,* "We saw the black hulk lying out a little way from the mud of the shore, like a wicked Noah's Ark". After the building of St Mary's prison in 1856 the hulks were scrapped, many of the timbers going into the houses built in Victorian times in Chatham and Gillingham. Another strange vessel laid up here, though not used as a prison hulk, was Brunel's massive steam/sailing ship the *Great Eastern* which, after laying the first trans-Atlantic telephone cable was moored here prior to being broken up in the 1880s.

A wonderful area for waders are these marshes with their banks of ooze uncovered at every tide, sanderling, dunlin, redshank and black tailed godwit, the last often moulting their plumage in August after the long flight from Iceland. Sheppey may see geese fly in during the autumn and winter, barnacle and grey lag among them. The study of the birds of the North Kent marshes is a subject all of its own and of considerable scope, with many books and articles being devoted to it and to the annual migrations which bring so many visitors. The upper reaches of our river also provide splendid habitat for ducks and many of the warblers, and great crested grebe often haunt the stretch between Wouldham marshes and Aylesford. In the higher reaches birds are mercifully more or less safe from pollution but there have been tragic losses down towards the mouth, in particular in September 1966 when an oil spill which happened while cargo pumping caused over 2,700 casualties, mostly gulls but several hundred waders including dunlin, redshank, oystercatchers and curlew. Also there were some wildfowl involved, notably mallard, pintail, pochard, shelduck and red-breasted merganser; while cormorant, guillemot and a great crested grebe were affected too. It took a whole year for the marshes to cleanse themselves from the oil and the emulsifiers.

Crossing the new Kingsferry bridge brings us finally to the Isle of Sheppey, the old towns of Queenborough and Minster, the thriving port of Sheerness and the holiday centres at Leysdown and Warden's Point. We are still really within the great joint estuary of the Thames and Medway yet the tang of salt is in the air as the fresh winds blow in off the sea, and the Medway estuary here is wide too. Despite vast oil tankers at Grain on the opposite shore, the many works and factories making glue, fertilisers and glass we are standing on the steps of history at Queenborough. There was a well-known factory making copperas here and at an early date, as Lambarde (the well-known Elizabethan historian) wrote in 1579 as follows, "I found there one Matthias Falconer (a Brabander) who did (in a furness that he had erected) trie and drawe very good brimstone and Copperas out of a certain stone that is gathered in great plenty upon the shore unto Minster in this Isle."

This substance used as a dye for woollen cloth, and tanning, was made by a simple process from iron pyrites. The pyrites was steeped in wooden vats for about six years after which the liquor was drawn off and boiled up. In the end,

**Great Expectations*

after evaporation one was left with crystals of the dye. There was another less important copperas works at Gillingham which has left its name in Copperhouse Marshes.

This little place of Queenborough with its fine old Guildhall once had a great castle covering some three acres and built by order of Edward III. We can imagine that any fortress built to satisfy that experienced warrior would be strong and well situated, and as Henry Yevele was the architect this would certainly have been the case. It was circular in form, defended by a moat and wall with a circular keep within, supplied with water from a deep well; Edward III honoured the neighbouring village with the name Queenborough after his Queen Philippa, proclaiming it a free borough. In due time the castle became a residence of the Lord Warden of the Cinque Ports, Tudor royalty visited here, Lord Howard of Effingham gathered his ships for the action against the Armada. However by Charles I's time the castle had become dilapidated and in due course the stones were removed for building purposes; so there is little sign of it now. On the other hand, sandwiched between more modern buildings are some fine old houses and the Guildhall dates back to 1728. There is also Church House, which was formerly a residence of Lady Hamilton so we may imagine Lord Nelson visiting her there. Down by the waterside small boats are moored, the place seems pleasantly quiet despite all the surrounding factories, the massive stone tower of the church refers us back to the great days when it first became a residence of kings and queens.

Before we voyage on to Sheerness, we should take a quick look at inland Sheppey for this was where the famous firm of Short Brothers had its inception, at Eastchurch. Overlooking this site from its eminence on the other side of the island and providing a splendid view of the estuaries of Medway and Thames as well as of the whole extent of this fertile land is the great church of Minster, one of the most striking and historic Abbey buildings in this part of the county. Dedicated to St Mary and St Sexburga it stands up on the highest point of the island, a strange and impressive shape, the sturdy and buttressed fifteenth century tower at the west end of one of the two chancels, a most unusual arrangement.

Saint Sexburga who founded the Abbey was the widow of King Erconbert of Kent and being granted this land here established a convent for seventy-seven nuns, herself being the first Prioress. Attacked and looted by the Danes, the Abbey was seriously damaged but by the time of the Norman Conquest the nuns had returned and in due course the Abbey was reconstructed by Archbishop de Corbeuil. The present church incorporates portions of the original Abbey in the north wall.

By the time Thomas Cromwell's inspectors were making their inventory prior to the Dissolution of the Monasteries the sisterhood had shrunk to the Prioress and only eight nuns so it was closed in 1535. Much of the land on

Sheppey was the property of the Shurland family, the tomb of Sir Robert Shurland, Lord Warden of the Cinque Ports, being on the south side of the chancel. There is something strange about this monument for the feet of the figure rest on a fully accoutred knight and there is a horse's head alongside the effigy. The Reverend Richard Harris Barham explained all this in the *Ingoldsby Legends* referring to the horse Grey Dolphin and the soothsayer who foretold that Sir Robert's steed would be the death of him. The superstitious knight slaughtered his horse on the beach to get rid of the curse but walking the shore some years later happened to put his foot in the horse's skeleton jaws where the tide had uncovered the body, he cut his toe on the horse's teeth, blood-poisoning ensued and he died, paid out for his cruel killing of his faithful steed. Some little way eastward from the church is the ruined gate-tower of the Shurland family manor which passed into the hands of Henry VIII's treasurer Sit Thomas Cheyne—who doubtless had as tough an assignment as the Sir Thomas Boleyn previously mentioned. These Cheynes inherited all the Shurland lands through marriage and Sir Thomas also acquired, or possibly was granted a large proportion of the monastic lands after the Dissolution. It is recorded that Henry VIII and Anne Boleyn paid him a visit here; so again we find that merry monarch riding into the pages of our story. One of his great interests was the newly created Royal Navy and when he visited Queenborough or Sir Thomas Cheyne at Shurland it would be very natural for him to survey with his shrewd and calculating gaze the most likely means of defence for any ships overhauling or careening in "Jillingham Water": Queenborough Castle would take care of any enemy vessels impudent or feckless enough to risk attacking via the Swale, but how about the Medway mouth? For this reason he made a thorough survey of the nose of land now known as Garrison Point at Sheerness and had a block house built here before 1537. It does not seem clear how long this existed or how effective it was considered to be, but by the time of Queen Elizabeth when the danger of Spanish attack from the Netherlands was assuming ever greater proportions a fresh survey was made and authorisation given for new fortifications. Unlike Queenborough, however, the place was not otherwise inhabited or used and L. Howard in the *Medway Ports Journal* suggests shortage of fresh drinking water as a perpetual problem on this site. There was however quite a lot of careening of ships, the men and their provisions of food and water being brought down by boat from Chatham.

All through the Cromwellian times the dockyard at Chatham was busy enough for under Admiral Blake the power of the navy was known and respected as far away as the Barbary Coast and Tangier. A very different picture evolved on the death of the Lord Protector for the Government rapidly became powerless, pay in the navy was hideously in arrears and it was with general relief that people learned that the Convention Parliament had asked

King Charles II to return. He immediately began looking into the possibility of establishing a dockyard at Sheerness, Samuel Pepys was sent down with instructions to prepare a detailed report on the feasibility of the scheme and, in the same year that the plague was causing so many deaths in the capital and throughout the land, major works were set in motion, and so the order came through for cleaning and refitting to be done at Sheerness instead of ships going all the way up the Medway to Chatham. A barracks, a repair yard and 26 gun battery at Garrison Point were part of the plan but progress was rather slow, and further surveys and additional work were still going on when De Ruyter and his Dutch fleet launched their assault. As will be appreciated, Sheerness was only just in being at the time, the defences were untried and, as we have seen, they collapsed in the face of vigorous assault. Work on the docks was put back years by the breaking down of sea-walls, the burning of the port and the flooding of the whole area.

The King spurred on repair work, Bernard de Gomme was given orders to increase the fortifications and His Majesty and Prince Rupert came down in 1668 to see how the work was progressing. They were not at all satisfied and further funds were made available with the result that when another conflict with the Dutch took place Sheerness was able to prove its worth as a repair and refitting base, and by 1689 ship building was also taking place. A graphic description is given in *Medport News* of the atrocious conditions endured by the fitters and men at the dockyard who had to live in converted hulks—the marshy air and swampy land causing a great deal of ague; and it traces back to those days the nickname "Sheernasty" so well known among service men. However despite many difficulties the dockyard was extended little by little, mud docks and wharves were made, and during the critical years of the eighteenth century and in the Napoleonic Wars it proved its worth as an admirable base for refitting and repair of the Nore fleet. Further hulks were sunk to act as break-waters, schemes for reclamation of saltings to be used for extra store-houses were embarked upon and in 1813 with the resources of the yard strained to the limit, John Rennie was given the task of producing an entirely new dockyard with all the associated administrative buildings. He and his son worked on a most daring and original plan supervising the construction of the Great Basin 63 feet wide at the entrance and with three dry docks, the whole built upon a foundation of soft mud and loose sand, an amazing engineering feat. The original working model from which the reconstruction of the dockyard was carried out and which was prepared with such exactness so that the illiterate English and French convicts employed on the work should understand directions came into the hands of the Medway Ports Authority in 1969, but because of its size it was not possible to put it on public display. However the Department of the Environment were interested and arranged to re-construct it in the Old Block Mills near H.M.S. *Victory* at Portsmouth.

The Sheerness of the present day seems far removed from all this. "Blue Town", the area originally connected with the naval dockyard, has seen a great change take place in the work going on here as, due to a programme of rationalisation, the naval yard was closed in 1960, the wharves and basins passing into commercial use. At Garrison Point the old Medway Conservancy Board realised the need for an up to date operations centre owing to the increased amount of commercial tonnage using the port and the Isle of Grain wharves opposite. This has been extended and improved by the Medway Ports Authority so that now, mounted in a purpose-built look-out position on top of Garrison Point fort, the Port Operations room commands a fine view of the estuary and as far up-river as Kingsnorth. Perched some 75 feet above sea level there is a clear view of some ten nautical miles, while the radar scanner on the mast above provides full coverage at night or in hazy conditions. This is very necessary when one reflects that some forty or fifty vessels a day pass in or out of Garrison Point.

The Great Basin referred to above has now been reclaimed, the area

The *Helen Turnbull* under way with the inshore lifeboat following in her wake. The heavy industry of the Medway mouth is clearly visible in the background.

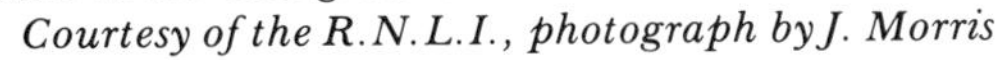
Courtesy of the R.N.L.I., photograph by J. Morris

concerned providing huge new storage sheds for imports and exports handled by Forest Products. There has been a demolition of the old Quadrangle store house inshore of the area of the former Small Basin, this to give additional space for container storage and handling, and of more immediate interest to those wishing to travel on the continent, the ferry service Sheerness to Flushing continues in full and vigorous operation. The ferry terminal has been moved a short way to give better access to the Inner Basin and Dry Docks area and to extend the space for fruit and general cargo handling. Also the barge-carriers known as LASH* come in to deliver their smaller 'children', and the Crescent group has developed a special pusher-tug *Lashette* for easier handling of these. So from the days of a busy naval dockyard Sheerness has now become a vivid and active port.

It is only comparatively recently that the Royal National Lifeboat Institution decided to station a lifeboat here, for most of the Thames Estuary work had been handled previously by the lifeboat at Southend. However with the change in coastwise cruising and dilapidations, there were doubts about the future of Southend pier where the lifeboat was housed, so the RNLI stationed a 40 foot lifeboat the *Ernest William and Elizabeth Ellen Hinde* (ON 1017) here at Sheerness on evaluation trials. She was an unusual boat, being the first R.N.L.I. craft to be moulded in Glass Reinforced Plastic and the number of calls soon showed that a Lifeboat Station here would fulfil an urgent need.

In 1971 the decision to establish a permanent station was confirmed and after a spell when Sheerness was operated by an older lifeboat the 46 foot × 12 foot 9 inch Watson design *Gertrude* (ON 847), the very much faster 44 foot *Helen Turnbull* (ON 1027) came here in 1974. Between 1969 and the end of 1979 186 lives were saved, and a further 51 by the inshore lifeboat. It was in the *Helen Turnbull* that Coxswain Charles Bowry carried out a notable service to the yacht *Eladnit* in 1975 which resulted in his being awarded the Bronze Medal for gallantry.

However this service took place out in the Thames Estuary, on the West Barrow Sands. That the Medway itself can provide hazardous conditions will be seen from the more recent service carried out on the night of 30th December 1978 and which resulted in the Coxswain being awarded a bar to his Bronze Medal. To conclude our survey of the river I cannot do better than to recount the events of that fateful night of gale and snow. At 8.46 in the evening the coastguard informed the lifeboat authorities that a red flare had been sighted in Gillingham Reach. The maroons were fired, the crew were hastily mustered and *Helen Turnbull* was under way shortly after nine o'clock. The night was heavily overcast, there were flurries of snow driving in on the northeasterly gale and the seas were very rough and breaking over the banks which were just covering as it was about four hours before high tide.

*So called from the initial letters of "Lighters Aboard Ship". The idea originated in America to cut down the length of time that sea-going vessels were immobilised in harbour and a feature of the LASH ships is the huge gantry or crane which hoists the lighters into the water where they are secured to buoys etc. ready for removal by tug at some later date.

Moving at three quarters speed because of the appalling weather conditions, *Helen Turnbull* was approaching the neighbourhood of the flare sighting at about 9.37 p.m. In the meantime news had been received that a yacht the *Ma Jolie II* was overdue on passage between St Katherine's Dock and the Medway. Coxswain Bowry fired off a parachute flare to give watchers an idea of the lifeboat's position and so that they could report if he was near the area of the original signal; and at 9.45 p.m. he received news that he was in the vicinity. With the direction of the gale, the tide and the run of the seas he knew that the yacht must be drifting in a southwesterly direction, so with all crew members on watch and with the searchlight stabbing the night through the heavy and continuous snow Coxswain Bowry headed *Helen Turnbull* up Pinup Reach: suddenly a small white light was seen, flashing S.O.S. from the Cinque Port Marshes just near the position of an old wreck and among some yacht moorings.

He could not tell the condition of the casualty, there were moorings everywhere, and he did not want to risk a moment's delay, so Coxswain Bowry decided to head straight in instead of veering down on his anchor. With his crew trying to con him clear of the moorings which were only dimly visible in the searchlight he swerved *Helen Turnbull* in and swung her head to sea about 15 feet away from the casualty, having to use the full power of his engines to turn her. The snow was driving down heavily, the flakes streaming horizontally in the Force 9 gale, the spray in the shallow waters was driving clean over both boats. For a moment he held her there, just long enough to find out that it was indeed the *Ma Jolie II* with two men on board, then he took the lifeboat clear to plan his approach. From her position he felt certain that the yacht must have struck the wreck which would be on the far side of her so he took the lifeboat in again, swung head to wind and eased her starboard side in to the casualty. A quick heave and a scramble and they had one man off but the lurching of the boats had swung them close to the moorings and the Coxswain had to run clear. After a moment's pause he went in again. A quick snatch, a heave, they had the other man.

At 10.20 the two survivors were landed at Gillingham Pier then the lifeboat faced the rough trip back against tide and gale, groping through the blinding snow till she was safely back at Sheerness. Before midnight she was berthed again and ready for the next call.

So we have brought this story of the Medway from the quiet rills of the Weald through stirring scenes and passing years, through locks and bridges to the wild breakers that test courage and seamanship to the limits, to the great waters where the ocean-going ships pass to and fro under the watchful eye of Garrison Point.

Bibliography

Archaeologia Cantiana—Many volumes.
Thomas Balston. *James Whatman, Father & Son,* Methuen 1954. *William Balston, Paper-maker.*
Hugh Barty-King. *Quilt Winders and Pod Shavers,* Macdonald & James, 1979.
C. W. Chalklin. *A Kentish Wealden Parish.*
W. Coles Finch. *Medway River and Valley. Windmills and Watermills,* Meresborough Books.
Daniel Defoe. *A Tour thro' Great Britain,* 1762.
Furley. *The Weald of Kent.*
John Forster. *Life of Charles Dickens,* Hazell, Watson and Viney.
Shephard Frere. *Britannia,* Routledge and Kegan Paul, 1967.
Dorothy Gardiner. *Companion into Kent,* Methuen, 1946.
R. H. Goodsall. *The Medway and its Tributaries,* Constable, 1958.
Edwin Harris. *Riverside History of Kent,* 1719.
Dr John Harris. *History of Kent.*
Edward Hasted. *History and Topographical Survey of the County of Kent,* 1782.
J. M. Harrison. *Birds of Kent.*
Roger Higham. *Kent,* Batsford, 1974.
Charles Igglesden. *Saunter through Kent,* 1928.
Samuel Ireland. *Picturesque Views of the River Medway,* 1830. *Medway Bridge,* 1793.
F. W. Jessup. *Kent History Illustrated,* Kent Education Committee 1966.
William Lambarde. *Perambulations of Kent,* 1576.
I. D. Margary. *Roman Roads in Britain. Roman Ways in the Weald,* Phoenix, 1948.
Donald Maxwell. *Unknown Kent,* 1921.
Arthur H. Neve. *The Tonbridge of Yesterday,* Tonbridge Free Press, 1932.
Samuel Pepys. *Diary.*
R. Hugh Perks. *Sprits'l,* Conway Maritime Press.
J. M. Preston. *Industrial Medway,* North Kent Books. *A Short History,* North Kent Books.
Joan Severn. *The Teston Story,* Rufus Fay Publications.
W. S. Shears. *This England,* RBC, 1937.
R. Southey. *Life of Horatio, Lord Nelson,* Dent Everyman, 1906.
Dr A. H. Shorter. *Paper Making in the British Isles,* David & Charles, 1971.
E. W. Straker. *Wealden Iron,* 1931.
V. Sackville-West. *Country Notes,* Michael Joseph, 1959.
Teignmouth Shore. *Kent,* A. & C. Black, 1907.
E. C. Talbot-Booth. *Ships and the Sea,* Sampson Low, 1938.
Alan Villiers. *The Way of a Ship,* Hodder & Stoughton, 1954.
F. C. Willmott. *Bricks and Brickies,* Private, 1972.
K. P. Witney. *The Jutish Forest,* Athlone Press, 1976.
M. Wyllie. *We Were One,* G. Bell, 1935.
Various authors. *Yalding.*

Also: *Bygone Kent; Coast & Country; Kent life; Kent,* the Journal of the Association of Men of Kent and Kentish Men; *Sea Breezes; Journal of the Council for Kent Archaeology; The Navy Year Book.*

Index